la leche league international

how weaning happens

diane bengson

Schaumburg, Illinois

To my family—John, Shaun, Joel, and Emma

 La Leche League International
1400 N. Meacham Road
Schaumburg, IL 60173-4840 USA
www. lalecheleague.org

First printing, June 1999
Second printing, January 2000
Third printing, March 2000

contents

chapter 1 • thinking about weaning

Shelly is sitting in her family room breastfeeding her six-week-old baby. Breastfeeding required some adjustments in the early weeks: getting the baby positioned well, dealing with leaking milk, and adapting her own life to nursing every couple of hours. But now she has cleared these hurdles—except that she's returning to her job in three weeks. Shelly enjoys breastfeeding, but is thinking she needs to wean.

Natalie's daughter, Juliette, is celebrating her first birthday on Saturday. While Juliette has begun eating some solid foods in her highchair, she remains enthusiastic about breastfeeding. To Natalie, Juliette still looks and acts like a baby, but her pediatrician says it's time to begin weaning.

Jeanne wants to wean her eighteen-month-old daughter, Tina. She wants to wean her gently and is willing to do whatever she can to make the process go smoothly, but she is uncertain how best to go about bringing a gradual end to breastfeeding.

Pam's son, Tyler, is three-and-a-half and rides his tricycle at breakneck speed. Most people don't realize he's still nursing, and Pam is sure that she's the only one in the neighborhood who is nursing a child big enough to talk about it. She's not enjoying nursing as much as she did when he was younger, but neither is she certain she wants to initiate a struggle over weaning.

Shelly, Natalie, Jeanne, and Pam recognize that breastfeeding is a way that mothers transmit both good nutrition and love to their babies and toddlers. This can make weaning a confusing issue, since it involves both a change in the food source, and a change in the mother-child relationship.

These mothers are concerned not only about how and when to wean, but also how to accomplish it with respect for each child's needs and for their own needs as well.

As a breastfeeding mother, you may have made decisions about when your baby would wean even before he was born, and you may have revised this decision several times since then. It's common for questions about weaning to surface again and again as a baby grows older. Mothers often wonder when the baby they are nursing will actually wean. This book will help you find answers to the question of when weaning will be best for you and your baby. It will also help you decide how to wean.

Shelly, Natalie, Pam, and Jeanne are all at different stages in their lives with their children, but they share many of the same concerns. These may be your concerns too. While this book offers no single solution for every weaning situation, its goal is to help you arrive at answers that feel right for you, your baby, and your family.

Weaning Basics

Weaning can happen in many ways, but weaning methods fall into four basic categories: abrupt weaning, planned or gradual weaning, partial weaning, and natural weaning. Here is a brief overview of each method.

Abrupt weaning means a sudden end to breastfeeding, with no warning or pre-planning. Some situations make this unavoidable, but whenever possible, mothers should try to wean more gradually. Abrupt weaning is difficult for both mother and baby. Because breastfeeding is the baby's source of comfort and closeness as well as food, a sudden, forced weaning is emotionally traumatic for the baby. Meanwhile mothers experience the physical discomfort of engorged breasts and risk a possible breast infection. The sudden shift in hormones associated with abrupt weaning may leave some women feeling sad and depressed for a time, especially if they were not comfortable with the idea of weaning.

In a planned or gradual weaning, the mother encourages the child to wean by providing interesting distractions and other nourishment in place of breastfeedings. The mother eliminates one feeding every few days, giving the baby or child plenty of other loving attention while they both make the transition from nursing to other forms of nutrition and comfort. The mother may offer other food and beverages more often, and may read to or play with her child in place of nursing. When weaning happens over a period of a few weeks or months, the child is less likely to be distressed and the mother is less likely to suffer from engorgement or sudden hormonal shifts. A mother may choose a planned, gradual weaning when she wants to wean but her child does not seem ready to wean on his own. When planned weaning is accomplished gradually and lovingly, it can be a good solution for many mothers and babies.

Mothers who try partial weaning are looking for a compromise between nursing a toddler frequently and weaning entirely. With this method, a mother gradually eliminates most nursings but continues to nurse her child once or twice a day. Often a mother chooses to keep the nursing sessions that her child relies on most, such as the one before sleep or immediately upon waking. A mother may also choose to eliminate the nursing sessions that are the most difficult for her, such as during the night.

Natural weaning means allowing the child to outgrow nursing on his own timetable. La Leche League's book THE WOMANLY ART OF BREASTFEEDING describes the philosophy behind this approach: "We believe that ideally the breastfeeding relationship should continue until the baby outgrows the need." Many mothers choose this approach because they recognize how important breastfeeding is to their child, or because they find it easier to wait for the child to wean himself. However, this doesn't mean the mother has no influence in the process. Natural weaning incorporates the natural limit-setting that babies need as they grow into toddlers. A mother who is practicing natural weaning views weaning as a developmental skill, and lovingly guides her child as he learns the skills that replace nursing. This guidance may involve asking the child to wait to nurse, or providing food or stimulating activity in place of nursing. It involves respecting the mother's feelings and preferences about breastfeeding while also taking into account the needs of the child. At the heart of natural weaning is this idea, expressed by Eda LeShan in *How Do Your Children Grow*:

We have to understand that when a need is met, it goes away. When they are finished with it, they will give it up. Sometimes it may go on longer than we expect, and a parent will worry because a 16-month-old is still nursing. This is a very natural tendency. We think the things that are happening will go on forever. The truth is that they will go on only as long as they are needed.

When Does Weaning Happen?

How long should breastfeeding go on? When should weaning begin? It may help to look at weaning as a process, not an event. Seeing weaning as something that will happen gradually over a period of months or even years, rather than as an overnight change, may be a new idea to you. Many

natural weaning means allowing the child to outgrow nursing on his own timetable.

mothers find that hurrying or trying to control the weaning process is stressful for themselves and their babies. They choose, instead, to be attuned to the needs and growth of their child so that weaning progresses at the child's pace.

The age when weaning happens is influenced by many factors. Your life circumstances, your baby's needs and personality, your needs and feelings—all of these figure in your baby's unique weaning timetable. Some children nurse longer due to their intense or sensitive natures, their strong sucking needs, or their need for a great deal of physical and emotional contact. In some cases, a child may nurse longer because of an unrecognized allergy or other physical problem. Sometimes weaning happens because the mother is ready to wean and gently encourages her child to do so. What is most important is that you meet your individual child's needs in the ways that are best for both of you.

Weaning can be seen as a lesson in trust. Trusting that your child will wean when he's ready is an act of faith, as is trusting that you and your child can find gentle, acceptable ways to wean. If you have never weaned a child or witnessed a natural weaning, or if your child is nursing much longer than you ever expected, it may be hard to believe that he will ever wean. But all children do wean! Watching your child wean as he is ready is wonderfully reassuring and can contribute to being able to trust your child in other matters in the future.

Heather Harlan Bacus, from Illinois, shares how she learned to trust in her child's ability to know when to wean:

Several years ago I took my son Micah, then five years old, and daughter Robin, three, to a playground. One piece of play equipment was a wooden balance beam positioned several feet off the ground.

While Micah busied himself on the jungle gym, Robin wanted to try her balancing skills. I stood with her as she hovered on the end of the beam. She reached for my hand and instructed me with a weighty glance, "Now Mom, don't you let go first!"

She was right. I had to trust Robin's capacity for knowing when she had her balance. What panic it might have caused her for me to let go first. Later, it occurred to me how weaning can be a lot like the balance beam.

In weaning, we learn to trust our little one's capacity to recognize the inner balance and emotional readiness necessary to relinquish closeness at the breast. I saw in a new light how putting pressure on a child to wean (consciously or unconsciously) before he's ready can be interpreted by that child as mother "letting go first." The result: a desperate, scary sense of losing something he feels he needs to face the world. He may cling even tighter at the mere prospect of the loss.

On the other hand, a few well-placed opportunities to offer a toddler an alternative activity or an outing with Dad instead of nursing may give him the courage to realize he's gaining his own "balance." Don't be mistaken: Your little one will let you know if he's ready for this step.

About halfway over that balance beam, Robin was no longer holding my hand. She was balancing herself and beaming with pride as she shouted, "Look Mom! I'm doing it myself!"

Funny thing. I never did notice who let go first.

Weaning—a Positive Experience

It can be tempting to see weaning as a cure-all, or as the surefire solution to whatever problems you and your baby are having. People around you, family, friends, or health professionals, may reinforce this view by suggesting that if you would only wean, things would be much better. Maybe you're feeling burned-out about nursing, or you must take a medication, or you're pregnant, and weaning seems like the only course open to you. Occasionally, weaning is the best and only answer. However, this book does not view weaning as the primary way to solve problems in the mother-child relationship. Instead, this book will help you to recognize the value of nursing in your life and your child's, and help you to find creative and personal answers to the challenges you face. This book provides ideas that will help you make weaning a positive experience for both you and your child.

Weaning from the breast is but one of the many "weanings" you and your child will experience together. How you wean, in and of itself, doesn't make or break your child for life. Your child's personality and your relationship are more complex than that. But taking weaning considerations to heart and carefully weighing your choices can teach you and your child a lot about the fascinating process of growing up.

Ideally, the way weaning happens for you and your child will provide a satisfying conclusion to a rewarding breastfeeding relationship. It can be like a surprising, revealing end to a good novel. Some mothers say weaning is like a joyous, but tearful, "bon voyage" at the beginning of a new adventure. Weaning signals the end of the breastfeeding relationship, but also a step taken in trust that the mother-child relationship remains close and significant for both of you.

> weaning from the breast is but one of the many "weanings" you and your child will experience together.

References

La Leche League International. THE WOMANLY ART OF BREASTFEEDING, 6th rev. ed. Schaumburg, IL: La Leche League International, 1997, 241.

LeShan, E. *How Do Your Children Grow?* New York: David McKay, 1972, 17-18.

Mohrbacher, N. *Approaches to Weaning* (pamphlet). Schaumburg, IL: La Leche League International, 1996.

chapter 2 • what natural weaning is like

"I think natural weaning is a good idea," Cindy said. Then she leaned toward her friend and whispered, "But quite honestly, I can't imagine Paul ever weaning himself! He likes nursing so much, he'll be nursing when he's in kindergarten!"

Many mothers breastfeeding today have not seen or experienced a natural weaning. They look at the child in their arms, nursing five or six times a day, and can't conceive of this little one willingly giving up such pleasure. Trusting that this child, like all children throughout history, will one day wean does not come easily in a society that views breastfeeding mainly as a food source for infants and expects that parents will control how and when the child weans. Looking ahead, finding out about what natural weaning can be like, both the joys and the difficulties, can help you have faith in your child and in your own mothering instincts.

Mothers who have already naturally weaned a child often are amazed at how weaning came about. Natural weaning is a complex dance between mother and child. Sometimes the mother leads, sometimes the child leads, sometimes they move in perfect synchrony with each other. Many mothers describe natural weaning as a cooperative venture.

Natural weaning doesn't follow a predictable course. Some children wean slowly and steadily, others seem to wean rather suddenly. Some children seem to be almost weaned for a very long time before they finally give up nursing for good! Mary Pierce of New York writes, "Natural weaning is not clearly defined but rather is a series of starts and stops, jolts, bumps, and side trips on the road to independence." It can be difficult not knowing when your child will wean, and it may seem as though you've given away too much of your parental authority by letting the child wean naturally. In fact, you have put the control over your child's development back where it belongs, in your child's hands. Weaning is a developmental issue, and as parents, we are far better off if don't try to control our child's normal course of development.

At the same time, natural weaning isn't about being the mother who nurses the longest or about entirely denying your own needs and limitations. Setting guidelines is a natural, necessary part of all aspects of your child's life as she grows older. You don't try to control when your child learns to walk or talk, but you do find positive ways to help her master these skills. In natural weaning, a mother guides her child toward weaning based on the limits the child is ready to accept. Cecily Harkins writes:

My own experience of nursing eight babies over a total of fifteen years bears out the realities of weaning. I am currently nursing two-year-old Morgan and have found I naturally delay or deny her nursing as she grows. I may have to drive a brother to Scouts or help an older teen with a project. Morgan is asked to wait a few minutes. I have no master plan to wean her, but I reinforce her ability to wait, to wait not only to nurse, but to wait to read a book, or to wait to do a puzzle, because instant gratification is no longer necessary for her maturation level. Although Morgan knows we no longer nurse at church I made an exception at the two-hour ceremony when her brother Luke was being confirmed. Flexibility and adaptation are part of weaning and growing up.

Natural weaning does require some surrender of control on the part of the mother. It seems to me similar to the surrender involved with preparing for natural childbirth. During pregnancy, I learned as much as I could, planned with my husband, took care of myself and my unborn child, and made my family and myself as comfortable as possible. I focused on the baby I was eagerly awaiting and took his or her needs into consideration. I believed that my body knew how to give birth. But finally, with each birth I walked into unknown terrain. When and how each baby arrived offered its own difficulties and delightful surprises. Natural weaning is much the same: we can prepare, plan, and trust, but ultimately the course of weaning is unknown.

Natural weaning can happen at many different ages, usually after the child has turned one year old. Our society is very number-oriented, yet much of the growth and many of the achievements of our children are not easily categorized by age. Parenting books or advisors may arbitrarily set age-related goals for different aspects of children's lives, from when they should sleep through the night and when they should read to when they should be ready to leave home. Yet many parents find that these particular ages don't necessarily match their child's readiness or abilities. Look to your child. Some children are ready to wean at eighteen months, some at three years. There is no one right age.

Natural weaning is an ideal, and like so many ideals, isn't always achievable. Unavoidable circumstances and the fact that life is far from perfect lead to many less-than-natural weanings. While natural weaning is an admirable goal for you as a mother, weaning in some other way does not mean you've failed, and it will not cause irreparable damage in your relationship with your child. What is most important is that you respond to your child with love, provide the emotional support your child needs, and maintain a close relationship with your child. Your life with your child is made up of many elements, and how you wean is only one of them.

Advantages of Extended Nursing and Natural Weaning

Many mothers choose natural weaning because they see many advantages to allowing children to nurse until they outgrow the need. Some of the advantages are due to the benefits of extended nursing, and others are due to the nature of natural weaning.

Benefits of long-term breastfeeding

Extended nursing, or nursing beyond the first year, is common in much of the world today and has been practiced throughout human history. Research confirms that breastfeeding's benefits extend past the age of one, and mothers report many advantages as well. Here's a summary.

Health advantages for children. Illness, including ear infections and diarrhea, is greatly reduced in breastfeeding children. Levels of antibodies and other immune factors in human milk actually rise as nursing continues past age one. As the mother's body gradually makes less milk, the immunities and nutrients become more concentrated. It is important for young children to continue receiving immunities from human milk, as their immune systems are not fully mature until around age six. This increased protection may be important to toddlers and preschoolers who are exposed to a wide variety of illnesses when playing with peers.

There are additional health benefits associated with longer breastfeeding. Nursing past one year enhances oral development, leading to less need for orthodontic treatment as the child grows. Breastfeeding can lessen the severity of allergies, or delay or prevent them. Breastfeeding contributes to better brain development. Extended breastfeeding also protects children from diseases like childhood cancer, juvenile diabetes, rheumatoid arthritis, and many others, and the benefits continue well beyond weaning.

Breastfeeding researchers have recently become more aware of the need to factor in how long a child is breastfed in relation to the extent of benefits. In nearly every study of this type, the longer the child was breastfed, the greater the benefit. Research has not yet considered breastfeeding in children past twenty-four months of age, but it makes sense that the benefits would continue, although they may diminish gradually as time goes on.

Continued nutrition. Human milk continues to supply significant amounts of fat, protein, and calcium in a child's diet, even past her first birthday. Human milk produced in the second year of life is nutritionally similar to human milk produced in the first year. It is still a high quality food. In fact, as the frequency of nursing decreases, the supply of immunities and nutrients in human milk becomes more concentrated. Toddlers may be nursing less than they did as infants, but they are still getting plenty of antibodies and nutrition.

Since toddlers are often picky and selective eaters, continued nursing can provide them with nutritious snacks and round out their diet. While breastfeeding alone is considered adequate for a child until sometime in the middle of the first year, your child will need additional nutrition by her first birthday. You will want to see that your child's diet includes iron-rich foods and a growing variety of fruits, vegetables, and whole grains.

Comfort in a busy world. Nursing is comforting for children. It helps them make transitions: from frantic to calm, from one activity to the next, from awake to asleep. Mary Frier Swisher from Michigan writes:

 Nursing was a wonderful way to connect with an exploring child. It also calmed both of us when the day was going less than smoothly. I can still hear that gasping sigh of contentment when a toddler would latch on and feel that all was right with his world once again.

A mothering tool. Many mothers who have nursed a toddler say nursing makes life with a toddler easier. One mother said that when her child is upset, "Nursing works like magic." It allows a mother to sit down, cuddle an otherwise active child, and get the child to sleep easily. Nursing is something even an exhausted mother can do, and it soothes the child almost immediately. Susan Redge of Michigan writes:

I was pleased that out of our chaotic life I could take time to relax and nurse knowing that I could close my eyes and the plants would be safe, he wouldn't be cracking eggs on the living room rug, or having a tantrum, or doing any of the other things two-year-olds might do. I've had the thought countless times that it is nursing that soothes the savage beast.

Many nursing toddlers stay on a short tether, connected to mother, never wandering too far from their source of security. This may make them easier to watch and protect. Nursing guarantees regular one-on-one time with a toddler. Mothers employed outside the home feel nursing helps them maintain closeness with their child. In the words of Helen Roth of New Jersey, "Nursing kept refocusing both of us, mother and daughter, back on each other."

Nursing also helps to enhance a mother's intuition. Mary Frier Swisher describes how nursing helped her to understand her child: "Breastfeeding, for me, became a barometer of my toddler/preschooler's physical and emotional health. When he wanted to nurse more frequently, I knew something wasn't quite right and even though I might not know what was wrong, nursing would help to make it right."

Support for the ill child. Many mothers who responded to the survey used to write this book mentioned how glad they were to still be nursing when their toddler was ill. Even a vomiting child can absorb some nutrition from human milk, and several mothers believed nursing spared their child from dehydration and hospitalization. Cindy George of Michigan writes:

I nursed Alli through a bout of what I thought was stomach flu, and even after she vomited, she wanted to nurse. Later I learned a particularly nasty rotavirus was going around, and some children were hospitalized with dehydration! My neighbor's daughter refused to drink anything and had to be put on an IV. I was so glad to still be nursing, because Alli refused any other fluids, but managed to keep enough mother's milk down to keep hydrated.

Nursing was also cited as the best way to comfort sick children, helping them rest and providing immunities and good nutrition so they could heal.

Health advantages for mother. Lactating women have elevated levels of prolactin, which along with oxytocin, the hormone responsible for the milk "let-down," produces the feelings of relaxation that women associate with nursing. A recent study showed that lactation reduces the body's chemical reaction to stress. This hormonally induced sense of calm can greatly help mothers deal with the changes and behaviors typical of toddlers.

Many mothers experience reduced fertility when nursing past a year, with some women going as long as two years or more without menstruating. This saves mothers from the bother and expenses related to menstruation, and also reduces the chance they will conceive babies very close in age. Research has shown that longer breastfeeding may protect a mother from rheumatoid arthritis. Finally, there is mounting evidence that extended breastfeeding reduces the risk of breast cancer.

Children like to nurse. Many mothers find they continue to nurse their children simply because they ask to nurse and enjoy it so much. Rachel O'Leary of England says her now-weaned middle daughter "remembers how she felt warm and cozy falling asleep at the breast." Mothers find satisfaction in providing this wonderful gift to their child. Barbara Sturmfels of New Zealand writes:

> *Nothing can compare with the feelings of a mother and her toddler when that small person outgrows the need to nurse for primarily nutritional reasons and falls in love with everything else that the breastfeeding relationship stands for. I have some trouble explaining these joyful feelings to myself, let alone trying to explain to others what they may risk missing.*

Meets the child's need to suck. The sucking need is very real, because sucking is soothing to babies and children. This need does not leave most children until after age one, and often not until much later. It's common in the United States to see two- and three-year-old children sucking on pacifiers and bottles. One of the big differences with nursing is that mother is attached! (And mom can't get lost, spoiled, or dropped in the dirt.) Nursing provides the comfort of sucking in the context of a human relationship.

Building intimacy. Extended nursing helps to make a child confident and people-oriented. According to one study that evaluated the effects of breastfeeding and subsequent social adjustment in six-to-eight-year-old children, those who were nursed the longest were later perceived to have the best social adjustment. Nursing teaches a child to build close relationships and to trust intimacy and commitment to other people. Long-time La Leche League Leader Elizabeth Hormann comments on how society makes it difficult for a child to learn these lessons: "We are bent on weakening bonds in the name of growth and independence, then spend our adulthoods wondering why we have trouble getting close to other people." Extended nursing gives a child another opportunity to learn communication skills and respect for other people. She learns she can influence her mother to get what she needs, but also learns that her mother has needs and limitations. Many mothers of older children report that their nursing relationship led to continued closeness and understanding through the years.

A common characteristic I've noted in children who were nursed through toddlerhood is their kindness and concern for others. My daughter enjoys playing with dolls and stuffed toys and often carries one with her most of the day. It seems that she is primarily interested in nurturing the doll, not using it for comfort, because her source of comfort is me and nursing.

Advantages to natural weaning

Mothers who practice extended nursing frequently see natural weaning as an extension of this choice. Long-term nursing and natural weaning are part of a continuum, and one often flows naturally into the other. Here are some of the advantages to continuing nursing until a child weans naturally.

An easy transition for baby and mother. Most of the mothers who answered the survey for this book and who had practiced natural weaning said life didn't change much when their child finally weaned. They had already adopted new patterns for going to sleep and waking, for comforting, and for showing love. When families had to make some changes as a result of weaning, such as finding ways for a child to go to sleep without nursing, mothers found that it wasn't too difficult to adapt to new patterns with older children who could be reasoned with and comforted in many ways.

Allows the child to fulfill and outgrow her needs. Pediatrician Marianne Neifert writes in her book *Dr. Mom's Guide to Breastfeeding:*

> *Trust your own heart, and know that you are doing the right thing for your baby when you allow her to wean at her own pace... . Believe that by meeting your child's dependency needs now, you will foster even greater independence later.*

Helps mother to trust her child's development. Learning to believe that your child will wean when she is ready is wonderful practice for handling future developmental steps. My own weaning experiences with my sons have helped me be less anxious and more able to trust that when they're ready to do something new, whether it's ride their bikes without training wheels, learn to read, or spend a week at camp, they will do it. I have been able to relax and trust their very individual timetables, and waiting for readiness has paid off, since they have then been able to take the next step with confidence and strength.

An easy way to wean. Many mothers comment on how much easier it is to go along with the child's needs, rather than have to put energy into changing a resistant child. With natural weaning there is less stress for mother, who in other weaning situations might have to be vigilantly substituting other things and second-guessing her child's requests to nurse. Natural weaning can be a pleasant experience for both mother and child. Mary Frier Swisher of Michigan writes, "You let them go at their own pace, and there are no struggles or tears over wanting and needing something mother won't let them have."

Mothers feel more positive about weaning. For mothers who wean when their child is ready, there is a sense of closure and the reassurance that their child got as much from the nursing experience as she needed. Barbara Sturmfels of New Zealand writes:

When the child is satisfied, the child will wean, having had all the needs that nursing meets, met in full. There may well be other ways to meet these diverse needs than by breastfeeding, but the risks are that they may not be met so fully and that the child may not ever become aware that her "cup" was never quite filled. By allowing ourselves as mothers to respond to our children in this intuitive way, we regain the chance to refill our own cups as well, and we can hope with some confidence that our children will go on to give these gifts to their children in turn.

Also, with natural weaning, physical changes in mothers are gradual. There is no engorgement and a slower adaptation to decreasing caloric needs. Mothers who wean naturally escape the more dramatic hormonal shifts associated with a planned or abrupt weaning. These hormonal changes can intensify feelings of regret or sadness.

The child remains in a secure relationship with mother. Dr. George Wootan, in his book, *Take Charge of Your Child's Health,* takes the emotional impact of weaning very seriously: "To a child, mother-initiated weaning is rejection." While it is possible for mothers who are encouraging weaning to offer plenty of support to their child, it is far easier to avoid having your child feel abandoned in the first place. When a child knows she can nurse when she most desperately needs to, she feels secure.

Child feels she has a sense of control over her life. Believing you can make things happen, get your needs met, and not be rebuked for asking for what you need contribute to a child's sense of self-esteem and self-confidence. A child who is allowed to wean naturally has an opportunity to put these qualities into practice in her nursing relationship, so that she is more likely to grow into a confident, positive child and an adult who believes her lifelong needs will be met.

References

Altemus, M. et al. Suppression of hypothalamic-pituitary-adrenal axis responses to stress in lactating women. *J Clin Endocrinol Metab* 1995; 80(9):2954-59.

Bergstrom, E. et al. Serum lipid values in adolescents are related to family history, infant feeding, and physical growth. *Atherosclerosis* 1995; 117:1-13.

Brun, J. G. et al. Breastfeeding, other reproductive factors and rheumatoid arthritis: A prospective study. *Br J Rheumatol* 1995; 34:542-46.

Ferguson, D. M. et al. Breastfeeding and subsequent social adjustment in six- to-eight-year-old children. *J Child Psychol Psychiatr Allied Discip* 1987; 28:378-86.

Neifert, M. E. *Dr. Mom's Guide to Breastfeeding.* New York: Plume, 1998, 435.

Romieu, I. et al. Breast cancer and lactation history in Mexican women. *Am J Epidemiol* 1996; 143(6):543-52.

Shu, X.-O. et al. Infant breastfeeding and the risk of childhood lymphoma and leukemia. *Int J Epidemiol* 1995; 24(1):27-32.

Wolff, M. et al. Blood levels of organochlorine residues and risk of breast cancer. *J Nat Cancer Inst* 1993; 85(8):648-52.

Wootan, G. and S. Verney. *Take Charge of Your Child's Health: A Guide to Recognizing Symptoms and Treating Minor Illnesses at Home.* New York: Crown Publications, 1992, 124.

chapter 3 · stories of natural weaning

Natural weaning can happen in many ways, and it is impossible to know exactly how the process will go for you and your child. The following stories reflect a variety of experiences with natural weaning and different feelings and attitudes in the mothers and children who have followed this course. Reading the stories will give you an idea about how natural weaning works and may give you ideas to try with your child.

Weaning at the Child's Pace

Many mothers find that weaning happens easily when their child is ready. Often, it's a matter of waiting while a child matures. Carol Becker of New York writes about this:

 My son stopped nursing last month. It was a momentous occasion celebrated with a new toy and a small "congratulations" party, complete with chocolate cake. For me, it was proof positive of the message: that babies and children grow and change at their own pace. It was this knowledge that helped me through some mighty intense times as the first-time mother of a child with high needs.

Fortunately, I found La Leche League meetings and publications invaluable in helping sustain me through the rigors of raising a poor sleeper and marathon nurser. At my first LLL meeting, when John was three weeks old, I found a copy of Dr. Sears' book THE FUSSY BABY. I did not buy it then because I did not want to admit that I had a fussy baby. However, I bought it at the very next meeting and read it at least ten times during those first two years.

I found that unrestricted nursing and almost constant physical contact were a necessity with John for the first three years. As difficult as it was coping with his round-the-clock needs, it was always easier to respond promptly to him than to try to make him less dependent on me by ignoring him. John just needed a tremendous amount of contact, love, attention, stimulation, and togetherness. Any slowdown on my part and he squawked loudly until I got it right. So, in this sense, John was a terrific teacher. He was determined to get his needs met, no matter what.

The wonderful thing now, as John approaches four-and-a-half, is the tremendous progress he has made, without tears or coercion. He loves his nursery school, he can comfortably stay with a babysitter, he sleeps in his own bed all through the night, and he can even play alone for short periods of time—all things I once thought I would never see happen.

Slowly dropping feedings, and going longer and longer between them, is a typical pattern for the natural weaning process. Many mothers who practice natural weaning say they don't remember their child's final nursing. Laurie Levy of New Jersey wanted to remember her daughter's last time:

I started out thinking I would nurse my daughter for six months exactly. It was nice to know that my La Leche League Leaders would be supportive no matter how long I chose to nurse. Those six months just came and went and before long I was nursing a toddler.

Eventually Kara was nursing about twice a day, usually morning and evening, but sometimes she would surprise me in the middle of the day or not ask at bedtime. When I became pregnant, I gathered information about nursing during pregnancy and nursing siblings and kept on nursing. Somewhere toward the end of my first trimester, Kara started to nurse less frequently—usually once a day and sometimes skipping a day here or there. I realized that she was really weaning, and I vowed to remember the details of the very last time she nursed and write them down so I would always remember the experience and someday share it with her. But sometimes she would skip a few days

and I would think that she had weaned and I couldn't remember anything about that last nursing. And then she'd ask to nurse again. This went on for a couple of weeks. Each time she'd nurse, I would forget to write about it, and then when several days went by and I was sure she had weaned I was so upset for not remembering that last time. Then something happened that I could not forget.

We had friends staying with us for the Fourth of July weekend with two very loud and active children. It was stressful for Kara, who is a mild-mannered little girl, accustomed to having things much quieter. After a whole day of running, yelling, and grabbing, she was exhausted. It was very late, and the other kids were still going strong. Kara was overtired and in tears. I finally scooped her up in my arms, carried her upstairs, lay down on the bed beside her, and held her. We could hear the other kids running around downstairs. Just as she was drifting off to sleep, Kara whispered, "Mommy, I need to nurse." And that was the last time.

Many mothers report that the end of a natural weaning process came suddenly. Rosemary Gordon of New Zealand tells about a surprise ending:

I nursed my second son until he was almost four. I do agree with those who say that a toddler won't choose to wean without some gentle persuasion from mother until at least the age of four. With my second son, I had no desire to exert any such persuasion—we didn't intend to have any more children and I was still very much in love with breastfeeding, having bottle-fed my first son.

Michael was still nursing two or three times a day up until he weaned so it was, for me, a very sudden weaning. He simply came into bed with me one morning to have his customary feed, opened my nightdress, then closed it again, saying, "No, I don't want it any more." End of story! I'm not sure what prompted this decision— maybe his six-year-old brother had been making comments on the fact he was still nursing, although I never heard it. However, Michael has grown up to be someone who has a goal and is self-motivated enough to work toward it without any prompting, so maybe he had an aim in mind, to wean at a certain time, and just did it!

Sometimes a natural weaning happens before the mother is expecting it to occur, and at a younger age than she had expected. Melanie Weiss of Illinois writes about her experience:

slowly dropping feedings, and going longer between them, is a typical pattern for the natural weaning process.

As my son approached his first birthday, he became a whirlwind. In fact, we named him Tornado Benjamin, because of the destruction that he would inflict on a room. Now cruising, he could reach all of those colorful objects that before had teasingly beckoned for his touch.

Suddenly, the breast was second best. My son no longer asked to nurse. Instead, at different times during the day—once in the morning and once in the afternoon—I would scoop him up from his play, settle comfortably on the couch, and ease him toward my breast. More often than not he would suck for a minute or two, then lose interest completely. At times he would playfully bite my nipple, reveling in my startled reaction. My stern face and the admonition "no biting" elicited from him a playful laugh.

Soon, my son went days without asking to breastfeed or being comforted by it when I initiated.

Months before, I had talked with a mother whose son had weaned himself from the breast at one year. I remember thinking to myself that my Benjamin will never self-wean at one year. Oh, what a struggle it will be to wean him, I had thought.

Breastfeeding for us began as it does for many women: with frustrations to overcome at first. Then, we settled into a pattern where breastfeeding becomes natural, easy. Soon I was nursing Benjamin in public: on park benches, inside a bank, in restaurants. What began with round-the-clock nursing whenever he cried turned into a comforting respite for us both.

As table foods were introduced at nine months, my husband would give Benjamin juice in a bottle. But mommy's warmth continued to win out over the bottle. At nine months Benjamin would breastfeed three or four times a day. At the breast, his eyes would lock dreamily into mine, registering sheer contentment. I felt my son's happiness down to my core, and his happiness became mine.

I was giving my son what he needed for the best possible start. During his first year, my husband and I had colds that came and went. While we blew our noses, Benjamin stayed healthy. "It's because of the human milk he's getting," I remarked a hundred-plus times.

I knew that my relatives, even my husband, were not in favor of the idea of Benjamin as a nursing toddler. But they respected our bond enough to accept it. I did care what others thought, but I also wanted the best for my child—don't we all? So I chose "baby-led" weaning, not expecting my baby to lead the way so soon.

The days after announcing Benjamin had officially weaned left me a bit fragile, and on one occasion I called my husband at the office and began crying. As time passed, I began to reflect on weaning as part of a wondrous cycle. By self-weaning, Benjamin was initiating the first of many separations. I should be proud of our son, I reasoned, for his display of independence, for his decisiveness.

I am sure there will be more milestones Benjamin will reach ahead of his mother! For now, we spend our days happily together. Breastfeeding may no longer be part of our relationship, but it is a big part of how we got to where we are now.

Weaning in the Course of Family Events

Natural weaning can happen suddenly and unexpectedly, due to an outside event or some major change in your family life. This is how it happened with one of my sons:

Shaun was still nursing at four. Since I was pregnant and nursing was becoming uncomfortable, I had encouraged him to nurse for shorter periods of time, and when he occasionally woke at night, he accepted being cuddled back to sleep. Still, he was very reluctant to give up nursing to sleep and on some days had moments when nursing was all that would comfort him. I assumed I'd still be nursing him after the baby was born, and this seemed okay to me since Shaun didn't nurse often.

His brother, Joel, was born at home when Shaun was four-and-a-half. Shaun was at home during the birth, with my sister, Lynne, to keep him company. Joel was born around 6 PM, and Shaun was in the room while Joel nursed several times during the evening. When Shaun's bedtime came, I went into his room and lay down next to him, prepared to nurse him to sleep. Imagine my surprise when he didn't want to! He wanted me to stay with him while he fell asleep, but he refused to nurse. For the next week, he refused to nurse, though he seemed happy and comfortable otherwise. I reassured him he could nurse if he'd like to. He told me once, rather offhandedly, "Ma-ma (his term for nursing) is for Baby Joel."

Then one night when Joel was about a week old, Shaun woke up sobbing. I carried him out to the rocker in the living room, and he cried and told me he loved Joel but he missed having it be just "Mom and Shaun." I had tears in my eyes and held him and talked about how I missed that, too. We cried and rocked for some time, and when we had both cried enough, he asked to nurse. He nursed to sleep and I carried him back to his bed. He never nursed again.

Now that he's a young teenager, I can see how this weaning is so reflective of his personality. He's careful not to interfere with what he perceives to be someone else's territory, and he still cherishes one-on-one time with the people he loves.

Sometimes weaning happens due to changes in the mother's body during pregnancy, as Margaret Nardella of New York recalls:

As soon as our daughter, Mary, was old enough to speak, she began referring to nursing as "all done." The first time this happened she crawled over to where I sat, plucked at the front of my shirt, and said, "All done?" I was so surprised. Where had she come up with this term? Then it dawned on me. After each nursing I would end with "All done?" and Mary had assumed that the act of nursing was called "all done."

Mary was an avid nurser right from the start, so the term "all done" became part of our everyday vocabulary. It cropped up in some pretty humorous situations, too. At nine months Mary accompanied me to an orthodontic appointment. She was lying on my chest, almost in a nursing position, as I was reclined back in the dental chair. The technician was just starting to work on my braces when Mary said quite loudly, "All done?" Before I could answer, the technician patted Mary on the head and said, "Oh, no, honey, I'm not done, I'm just getting started." Another time, we were checking out at a store after a long wait, and Mary, getting antsy, wailed, "All done!" At this, another shopper leaned over and said, "My children are just the same, always asking, 'Are we done yet?'" These incidents made me laugh because only Mary and I knew what was really going on.

As Mary grew, she continued to nurse, and I was happy having a contented, well-adjusted nursing toddler. When her third birthday came and went, however, I admit I did wonder if she would ever be "all done"! I looked to my wonderful La Leche League Leader, Eileen, as a model. Her daughter, Allyson, was about ten months older than Mary and still nursing. When Allyson weaned at almost four-and-a-half, I realized that Mary would also wean eventually. I was content to let Mary be the guide in the weaning process.

I became pregnant when Mary was three-and-a-half, and the advice from my doctors was to wean. I checked with Eileen, and she told me that there was no known threat to the fetus if I were to continue nursing Mary, even up to and after birth. She also said that pregnancy is a practical, natural time to wean an older nursling, which made me feel better. I decided to reduce Mary's nursings to two each day, naptime and bedtime. Although Mary said several times that she didn't like the deal, she was cooperative. I knew giving up some of her nursings was a big step for her since she had told me many times that "all done" was her favorite thing.

When I asked Mary when she planned to stop having "all done," she said, "When I'm four." To her, that was a long way off when in truth it was only about six weeks away. I knew I didn't have the heart to enforce this, and, as it turned out, I didn't have to. Soon after that, when Mary was nursing, she stopped after a few sucks from my left breast and said there was nothing coming out. Then she switched to the other side. When I asked if there was anything there, she nodded emphatically. Next morning I asked Mary again if there was any milk. She looked at me rather sadly and admitted, "No." I took her in my arms and held her close. I told her she was growing up and that even though we weren't having "all done" anymore, I still loved her very much, and we could still be close whenever she wanted. We agreed to read a book before her nap and at bedtime as a substitute.

I'm so proud of my daughter. I think weaning marks the greatest step so far in her growth and maturing. I'm glad Mary nursed as long as she did because I think she'll be able to remember this special part of her childhood, this thing we fondly called "all done."

Sometimes weaning seems to happen by accident, though it might be more accurate to say the child was ready to wean and the outside circumstances merely allowed weaning to happen. Janet Mann of New Jersey tells about this kind of weaning:

After watching my La Leche League Leader with her nursing three-year-old, I decided to allow my son to wean when he was ready. Because of a long struggle with infertility and the probability that he would be our only child, I felt I wanted to fully experience nursing with him.

Weaning was so gradual that I never really thought about it or realized that feedings were decreasing as solids and activities were increasing. I actively encouraged bedtime weaning at age two-and-a-half because I still had an outside hope of conceiving again and wanted to see if it was possible. He was waking up three or four times a night, and I wanted him to develop a better sleep pattern. I lay down in his bed with my back to him, so he could cuddle up to my back and put his arm around my neck. I talked or sang quietly for five minutes, then lay there silently until he fell asleep. It took several months, but eventually he learned to sleep through the night.

By the time he was three years old, we were pretty much down to nursing once a day, first thing in the morning. When he was three-and-a-half we had a change in our routine due to a death in the family, and he didn't nurse for two weeks. He sort of weaned by accident. Occasionally afterwards he asked for "nursies," but more out of curiosity than any real need and accepted it when I explained they "didn't work anymore."

Recognizing Steps toward Weaning

Some mothers take advantage of a child's declining interest in nursing to help weaning move along a little faster. Christine Patrick of New Jersey writes:

On her own, Chelsea had begun nursing mornings and nights only. After a while, I felt it was a good idea to stick with this pattern. If she wanted to nurse at other times I'd say "We nurse mornings and nights now." She agreed to that. If she had been upset or really seemed to need to nurse I would have nursed her. But she must have been ready because it really wasn't an issue.

Weaning was very gradual. She stopped nursing at three years, two months, at which time I was three months pregnant. She just decided she didn't want to nurse anymore. She preferred other things to nursing. She tells me (six months post-weaning) that she loves her "nurse-nurse," and once, about six weeks after she had nursed for the last time, she said she missed her "nurse-nurse," but she has never asked if she could nurse again (which I thought she would do).

Quite often natural weaning is a combination of the mother suggesting weaning steps at the time the child is ready to accept them. Nancy Turnbull of Great Britain writes about how she learned to follow her daughter's cues:

I found that although I tried to guide my daughter toward weaning, progress came naturally, in its own good time. Sometimes I made mistakes and tried things when my daughter was obviously not ready, for example, when I tried to get her not to nurse every time she woke at night. Nothing I did worked until she was about two-and-a-half. Maybe it's because I am lazy. With night nursing, I'd say to myself "Tonight we'll try not nursing" so I'd walk her and sing to her and she'd become wide awake. So I'd say "Forget this—I want my sleep," and we'd go back to nursing at night. I made no further effort to encourage her not to nurse at night for four to six months, then discovered she was happy to have me just lie down with her while she went back to sleep. Perhaps if I had been more sensitive to her cues, she would have given up night nursing sooner. On the other hand, if I had not introduced her to the idea of not nursing at night, it might have gone on longer (she still comes into our bed during the night).

We had a talk about nursing frequently during the day, and I suggested that maybe we could just nurse when she was tired, in her room. This worked very well. She had been nursing often during the day; it seemed to be for two reasons. First, nursing was a way of enjoying my attention and being reassured by my presence. Second, it

natural weaning is a combination of the mother suggesting weaning steps at the time the child is ready to accept them.

would help her to fall asleep when she was tired even if there was a lot of commotion going on around her. When we started going upstairs for nursing, she was almost three and was able to decide (most times) why she wanted to nurse. If she wanted to nurse for attention, she would come sit on my lap for a cuddle or we'd play. If she was actually tired, she would ask to nurse, and we'd go upstairs to sleep.

It was about six months later that she stopped nursing. She had forgotten about nursing in the morning, and the daytime nursings had stopped on their own, since she no longer took a nap. I suggested that at bedtime I could just lie down with her. She didn't mind this change, and that's what it's been ever since. She occasionally asks to nurse and when I let her, she nurses for half a second, I think just to know it's there!

Helping a Child Plan to Wean

Many mothers reported that their child needed help to take the final step in weaning. In some cases, the mother helped the child formulate a weaning plan. Barbara Sturmfels of New Zealand writes about her daughter's weaning by design:

When Leslie and I embarked on our nursing partnership, I would have been astonished and disbelieving if someone had looked into the future and told me that this stage of our relationship would last for a full five years. At the time of Leslie's birth, my thoughts were not at all focused on the weaning process (that was way in the future) and I find it difficult to recall just what my expectations were. I think that I expected to nurse Leslie to the point where she would be weaned onto food rather than formula or milk in a bottle.

What I was not aware of, perhaps could not have been aware of, was the complexity of a small child's needs and how essential my breasts would be to Leslie as a tangible, physical, "hands-on" manifestation of the mother-baby bond. She seemed to need the process of taking an actual product from my body and of my body giving it to her. It occurs to me that there is no way other than by breastfeeding that a mother can do this directly for her child. Other forms of physical contact provide physical safety and emotional nourishment but lack the product—mother's milk—which is taken deep into the child's own body. Other comfort foods and objects do not have the direct link to mother.

Leslie nursed long and often. It was a first-choice activity until she was around three years old. What another child might regard as an interesting and absorbing opportunity to try something new was perceived by Leslie as a stressful situation in which she needed protection. As Leslie approached four, her nursing needs declined but did not disappear, even though my supply virtually dried up due to pregnancy. After her younger brother Evan was born, her once-or-twice-a-day nursings became more rewarding and more pleasurable again, for both of us. (What a grand little fellow that baby was, bringing all this milk!) By about four-and-a-half, she had probably outgrown the need to nurse, and she would have coped comparatively easily with weaning. But she still derived considerable pleasure from her once-daily nursing, and I was happy to provide that pleasure. Her needs definitely did not have that urgency any longer—she no longer seemed to be trying to "climb back inside my skin" (these are words she once used to describe nursing—further evidence of her need for intense body-to-body contact). And so our "When I'm Five" contract was born.

The final weaning process was a negotiated settlement. The conversation would go something like this:

Me: When do you think you'll stop having "ba"?
Leslie: When I don't need "ba" anymore.
Me: When do you think that might be?
Leslie: When I'm five.
Me: You think you won't need "ba" anymore when you're five?
Leslie: No. School children don't have "ba."
Me: Don't they?
Leslie: No. That would be silly! Children go to school without mummies.
Me: You could have "ba" before school.
Leslie: No, I won't have "ba" anymore.
Me: Why not?
Leslie: Because I won't need "ba" anymore.

And so, with months of notice, Leslie prepared herself to finally wean. She had had a few temporary weanings along the way. For example, when she was nearly four and we were staying at Gran's for a few days, she agreed that she wouldn't nurse while we were there, because "Gran thinks I'm too old to nurse, but we don't, do we?" And while we were camping over the summer she'd often miss a day or two—I'd be out swimming before she was awake and she'd have forgotten all about her morning "ba" by the time our paths crossed again.

Leslie's last day of nursing was carefully planned—she was going to have one side in the morning and the other side in the afternoon *after her birthday cake. As the day approached, this plan had to be modified as she decided that she had to start school on her fifth birthday. So, as it happened she had her party and her cake two days before her birthday, and she did nurse after her cake (but graciously waited until after the guests had gone). The next day she nursed in the morning so that part of the plan was adhered to as well. And the final "whistle" came on her fifth birthday, the day she started school, when she woke up and climbed into bed with me, snuggled in, and attached herself to my breast with that blissfully contented look on her face and nursed for a full fifteen seconds. Then she suddenly detached herself, leaped out of bed, and ran down the hallway calling out "I've got to pack my school bag!"*

A new era had been well and truly heralded in.

Often part of a weaning plan is suggesting a point in the future, when the child will nurse for the last time. This works surprisingly often with older children. Terry Cater-Cyker of New York explains how weaning happened for her son:

When my first child was a toddler, my father, to whom all this breastfeeding stuff was new, was concerned that Mitch would still be nursing when he went off to kindergarten. I laughed and assured him that Mitch would wean before then.

Mitch nursed happily through my second pregnancy, with no signs of waning interest. Zachary arrived when Mitch was twenty-seven months old. Big brother generously shared his "me-me" with the new baby, and we continued as a nursing trio for quite some time.

Sometime after Mitch's fourth birthday, the topic of weaning came up, and together we agreed that four-and-a-half was a good age to wean. (Why was it a good age? I don't know, but all three of my children used half-year birthdays as goals for toilet training and weaning.)

As we moved toward that four-and-a-half year mark, Mitch gradually nursed less, mostly on his own initiative, with support from me. "Neither offer nor refuse" was a good approach for me to use with Mitch. We did have our "alphabet me-me" for times when the frequency of requests to nurse was overwhelming to me. Mitch could nurse as often as he liked, but the length of the nursing was determined by how long it took me to sing the alphabet. This not only helped me cope, but taught Mitch the alphabet, too.

When that four-and-a-half birthday arrived, we went through the usual bedtime routine. We talked about it being our last nursing. Mitch nursed as long as he wanted that night. When he was through,

he looked up at me and said, "Mom, that milk will last me forever."
Then he cuddled in and went to sleep.

Mitch went to kindergarten six months later, no longer nursing.

Finding a Way to "Let Go"

Sometimes a child is ready to wean, but needs help "closing the door." This
was the case with my younger son:

*Joel was still nursing regularly past age three. He was (and still is) a
high energy child who tends to act on impulse and not have much self-
control. Nursing was invaluable to him as a way of getting
"grounded" and feeling relaxed; for me it was a way to rest and a
chance to tenderly reconnect with him when I was tired and
exasperated.*

*About the time he was four-and-a-half (the age his brother
weaned), I began to talk about how he might be ready to stop having
"da" when he turned five. I only mentioned it occasionally and briefly
and wasn't expecting this to happen, knowing that self-discipline was
not Joel's strong suit. I did encourage him to nurse less often, and
continued to find new ways to connect with him that did not require
nursing.*

*On Joel's fifth birthday, after a nice family celebration, it was time
for bed. After I read to him, he said he didn't want to have "da"
anymore now that he was five. He seemed to think it was his own
idea, and I didn't contradict him. He didn't nurse again. I think he
was ready to wean, but needed a little encouragement. Also, I think if
I had been too pushy about weaning on his birthday, he probably
wouldn't have. He was proud of himself and has used other birthdays
since then to take big steps.*

Zena Sandy of Ohio tells how she helped her daughter take the last
step in her natural weaning:

*By the age of four my daughter, Jillian, was nursing just once a day,
usually at bedtime, and I expected that she would soon be totally
weaned. However, another year came and went and she was still
nursing once a day. I felt she was ready to stop nursing but didn't
know how to let go, and I wasn't sure how to help her.*

*One day we were visiting with a friend who had just retired after
thirty years as a kindergarten teacher. Jillian and I listened as Sue
told us how much she had enjoyed her work, how she would miss the
children, and also about her exciting plans for the future, including*

extensive traveling with her husband who had already retired. As she talked, I realized that retirement was also a weaning of sorts. Sue had devoted many years of her life to her job; now she was ready to let go of that phase and move on to a new one. "Just like Jillian," I thought, "except Jillian doesn't know how to retire." Then I had a brainstorm.

When we got home, I explained to Jillian that my nursies (breasts) had worked very hard over the last eight years happily feeding her and her sister, Heather; now they wanted to retire. Jillian thought about it. "Okay," she said. I couldn't believe it could be that simple and waited to see what would happen at bedtime.

Sure enough, she asked to nurse. When I reminded her that my nursies wanted to retire now, she smiled, then kissed each breast once, said goodnight, and went to sleep. After that, she asked to nurse a couple of times but was content with my reminder that my nursies were enjoying their retirement.

I'm still not exactly sure why this approach worked when nothing else had. I think the idea of my breasts retiring from nursing gave her a sense of closure and made it possible for her to let go of nursing completely. I had tried planning a weaning party with her, but that had not worked because, I think, from her viewpoint, my breasts had not changed their function and were still available for nursing. Telling her they were retired gave her a new perspective, and she was able to totally wean herself when she was ready, emotionally, physically, and intellectually.

chapter 4 • breastfeeding and weaning as your baby grows

Your relationship with your child is always growing and changing. Your breastfeeding relationship with your child will also grow and change. For example, a newborn may need extra help latching on, but by the time she's four months old, she's nursing like a pro, pausing only to smile up at her mother. At fifteen months, she can sometimes wait for a feeding, but she may want to nurse immediately for comfort when she stumbles and falls. As a nursing three-year-old, this child is too busy playing with the neighborhood children to nurse during the day, but at bedtime she seeks the comfort of the breast to help her fall asleep.

Just as breastfeeding is different at different ages and developmental stages, the weaning process is different, too. This chapter will help you see what weaning might be like at different ages and what factors to consider when weaning at a particular age. As you read through this chapter, bear in mind that your child's pattern of development is influenced by her personality and inner timetable and may differ from the descriptions given.

Newborn to Six Months

Babies up to the age of six months often breastfeed every couple of hours, with a longer interval during the night. It's amazing to watch your baby grow so much in the first months and realize it's because of the milk your body has given her! Many breastfeeding mothers enjoy the intimacy and closeness of nursing a baby at this stage. Still, you may feel as though you get little else done besides breastfeeding and caring for your baby. It can also feel overwhelming to be so needed by one person. This is all part of the nature of mothering a young baby, whether the baby is breastfeeding or not.

This is also a time of rapid change. Many mothers have found that their babies change from week to week at this age. Problems of last week, or last month, are nearly forgotten as the baby moves on to new developments and challenges. Getting the baby to sleep and mother's lack of sleep are often issues at this age. Sometimes the early months present difficulties like sore nipples, a fussy baby, or fears of not having enough milk. Some mothers feel ready to wean before the first six months have passed.

Weaning at this stage works best if it is gradual, and at this age babies will wean to bottles. Your doctor can help you decide what is best to feed your baby in place of mother's milk. Start by replacing one breastfeeding in a twenty-four-hour period with a bottle-feeding. After two or three days, substitute a bottle for a second feeding at the breast. With this method you will have weaned your baby to bottles in about two to three weeks' time. When you wean gradually, your milk supply will diminish slowly, and you are less likely to encounter engorgement or a plugged duct in your breast. Going slowly also helps your baby adjust to the change. Your baby may need additional sucking beyond the time spent drinking from the bottle and may choose her thumb, or you may offer a pacifier. Being especially loving with your baby during this time, holding her while she takes her bottle, and reassuring her of your presence will help weaning go more smoothly for both of you.

Some babies who have not encountered a bottle before may be reluctant to accept it initially. You may have more success at the beginning if someone else gives your baby a bottle, such as your partner, another family member, or a caregiver your baby is familiar and comfortable with. Try offering the bottle when your baby is neither too hungry nor too sleepy, perhaps before the baby's usual nursing time. Touch the bottle nipple to your baby's lips and let her take it into her mouth, rather than forcing it in. You may need to experiment with different types of bottle nipples to find which one your baby prefers. You or your helper can also experiment with holding your baby in different positions while feeding her. Some babies like to sit up with their back leaning against their mother's chest while taking a bottle. Others will accept a bottle if they're being rocked, walked, or swayed.

If breastfeeding isn't going well in the early weeks or months, weaning may seem very tempting. Consider waiting a while longer. Breastfeeding is something you and your baby are learning to do. It takes time to work out difficulties. Seek out additional help for your problem from a La Leche League Leader or a lactation consultant, from the LLLI book THE WOMANLY ART OF BREASTFEEDING, or from the suggestions in the chapter "Pressure to Wean." Sharon Parrish of Michigan writes about her early difficulties:

"Don't give up! It really does get better!" I heard those words over and over from my obstetrician and birthing center nurses, and later, too, from my La Leche League Leader. "Gets better?" I thought. "When?"

Between Sarah's crying, her problems latching on to my flat nipples, and my cracks, blisters, and soreness, I thought it would never work out! After a two-to-three week effort (with family members telling me that not all women can breastfeed and that Sarah was crying so much because she was hungry), I was ready to give up. I began introducing her to formula, which she took readily, though she preferred the closeness of my breast. For a while I was feeding her more formula than breast milk. She didn't seem to mind, and my sore nipples loved the time off. But at her one-month checkup, I was told that with all of Sarah's colicky symptoms she was probably allergic to cow's milk and the formula was only making matters worse.

I had gone around and around wondering what to do. Should I stop nursing altogether? Should I nurse and supplement with a bottle? Should I tough it out and make nursing work for us? Finally the decision was made for me. Sarah's pediatrician said if I was physically and psychologically prepared now to completely nurse my child and eliminate dairy products from my own diet, her health would improve.

Immediately I contacted La Leche League and began learning how to position Sarah effectively during nursings to help prevent soreness when she latched on. It was like a weight being lifted off my shoulders to know I was doing the right thing for my daughter. Not only was I feeding her the best nutrition available, but the doctor said it would also help her stomach pains and crying.

It wasn't easy, but we made it! Yes, it finally did get easier. I might never have stuck it out if I hadn't kept hearing the words, "It really does get better!"

If you do wean your baby during the first six months of her life, you can be reassured that your baby benefited greatly from the time she

if breastfeeding isn't going well, weaning may seem very tempting; consider waiting a while longer.

was breastfed. Even a few days or a few weeks of breastfeeding bring benefits that may last a lifetime.

Six Months to One Year

By age six months breastfeeding is well-established and familiar to mother and baby. Breastfeeding during the second half of the first year is often easier and more comfortable than it was during the early months. Babies may still nurse often, and nursing at night is still common.

The baby will be learning to eat solids during this time, though she may not be eating a wide variety of food during these months. Starting solids is the first step in weaning, but it doesn't necessarily mean that your baby will soon be ready to give up your milk. Human milk will still provide most of your baby's nutritional needs until she is about a year old. At first, each of your baby's meals of solid food should be preceded by nursing. This will ensure that your baby continues to receive sufficient amounts of the high-quality nutrition in your milk. Start solids slowly, in small quantities, with only one new food introduced each week. It helps to look at the first few months of eating solid food as a time of experimentation and learning, instead of a rush to get your baby to adopt grown-up eating patterns.

Older babies are more easily distracted during nursing. They may look around the room, turn their heads at the sound of other voices, or be unwilling to nurse unless they are in a quiet place. Some mothers take this as a sign that the baby wants to wean, but this may not be the case. Many mothers and babies have experienced this problem with being easily distracted and have gone on to nurse much longer, so it may be that baby's need is for extra help to concentrate on nursing rather than needing to wean. Mothers have found they can weather this period by nursing in quiet settings until their baby is more mature.

Sometimes a baby may suddenly refuse to nurse, and mother, after many unsuccessful attempts to get the baby to take the breast, concludes that this baby has weaned herself. Actually, this baby may be on a nursing strike, which is different from natural weaning. A baby on a nursing strike is usually not very happy, and her mother, surprised by the sudden disinterest in nursing, is not very happy either. Fortunately, with care and attention, most babies will resume nursing within a few days. For suggestions on persuading a baby to take the breast again, see the section "Is this weaning or a nursing strike?" in Chapter 10, "When Weaning Isn't Going Well."

Babies' first teeth often erupt during the second half of the first year, and some babies may bite during nursing. This problem is usually short-lived, and can be dealt with by gently removing the biter from the breast. Many mothers have found that babies who continue to bite often do so toward the end of a nursing or when they don't really want to nurse. A mother can avoid those situations by watching her baby for clues that she's going to bite and removing her from the breast before she clamps down. For more suggestions on teaching a baby not to bite while nursing see "When a baby bites" in Chapter 9, "Mother's Feelings about Weaning."

If you decide to wean a baby at this age, your health care provider can help you determine what kind of milk or formula to give your baby in place of human milk, as well as help you decide how much solid food is appropriate. It's important to go slowly. At first, replace only one breastfeeding per day with a bottle. After two or three days, substitute a bottle for another breastfeeding. You will find it best to replace nursing sessions with bottle-feedings, since your baby still needs to suck, but you may also choose to increase the amount of nutritious solid foods your baby eats. Watch your baby for signs that she is getting enough to eat and is not unduly upset by the process of weaning. Some babies who are close to a year old will wean to a cup instead of a bottle, but most continue to need some form of sucking. If you are weaning to a bottle, some of the suggestions about introducing bottles in the preceding section, "Newborn to Six Months," may be helpful.

While you are weaning, you may find that you need to distract your baby from the idea of nursing from time to time. This may require changing some of your daily routines, but it is best for you and baby if being away from one another is not a part of weaning. Your baby still needs to be held by you and to be with you as much as possible. She will benefit nutritionally and emotionally if the transition from breast to bottle is slow. It is not uncommon for a baby of this age to turn toward mother's breast or lie back across her lap and signal she wants to nurse, so you may need to find new ways to cuddle that don't remind the baby of nursing. Many babies at this age have become accustomed to falling asleep while nursing, and part of the weaning process will be learning new ways to go to sleep. Some of the ideas in Chapter 5, "Gently Encouraging Weaning," will be helpful to you.

Consider taking weaning quite slowly, dropping one feeding only every week or two, allowing weaning to take a couple of months instead of two or three weeks. There may be one or two special feedings each day that you and your baby will continue to treasure. Breastfeeding gives your baby a wonderful start in life, and weaning gradually and gently while reassuring your baby of your continuing presence will help both of you make this transition in a positive way.

your baby still needs to be held by you and to be with you as much as possible.

One-Year-Olds

Breastfeeding past the age of one often takes on a different character. Toddlers have many reasons to nurse. One reason is that they enjoy the familiar taste of their mother's milk when they're hungry. One-year-olds also find that mother's breast is a safe haven, a place to return to after a toddler-sized "adventure." They use breastfeeding for comfort and closeness and may often view nursing as the most enjoyable way to be with mother, especially after separations. They are usually eating a variety of foods, but some who are allergic or slow in starting solids may still depend on nursing for the majority of their nutrition. Toddlers usually prefer many small meals, and often like to eat "on the go."

Some children will wean naturally sometime before their second birthday, but often this does not happen. While no age guarantees that weaning will be either easy or difficult, a child between the age of one and two is often challenging to wean. Some mothers, seeing their little one's passion for breastfeeding, fear that their child will be this insistent about nursing for a long time to come. However, as a child develops other skills and abilities, nursing will gradually become less important.

Weaning at this age requires mother to be very available to her child in ways other than breastfeeding, and again, to take each step as slowly as possible. While a few toddlers may wean readily when other types of food and drink are substituted for breastfeeding, this is not the case with most one-year-olds. Weaning at this age requires liberal doses of distraction from nursing, and plenty of attention from mother. Offering drinks and snacks before or in place of breastfeeding may help to take the focus off nursing, but since toddlers nurse for reasons beyond hunger, weaning will also require finding ways to satisfy these other needs without nursing. Many toddlers respond best when mother substitutes other interesting shared activities for breastfeeding during the day. Weaning will also require changes in the family bedtime routine. See Chapter 5, "Gently Encouraging Weaning," for ideas that will work for your child.

Mothers of one-year-olds often don't mind the idea of continuing to nurse, if only their toddler would nurse less often. These mothers may choose to wean from the feedings that are most difficult for them, while continuing to nurse at the times of the day when breastfeeding is most comforting to their child or at the times when it is most convenient to them, such as before bed or early in the morning.

Some mothers wean when their child is a year old because they've been told their milk is no longer good or no longer serves any nutritional purpose. Be assured that your milk is still as good for your baby as it was during the first year of life. In fact, your milk has changed to meet the specific needs of older nursing babies and children. When your child nurses less frequently, the immunities in the milk are more concentrated. Studies have shown breastfed toddlers to be healthier than their bottle-fed peers.

Other mothers feel pressure to wean because they don't know anyone who has nursed past one year. It can be helpful at this point to read more on the subject, or to seek out mothers who are nursing older babies. Often these mothers are found at La Leche League meetings or other settings where nursing mothers gather.

Two-Year-Olds

Two-year-olds are even busier exploring their world than one-year-olds. They often nurse less than they did at one, and may be better able to accept the idea of waiting to nurse. Children at this age still find great comfort in nursing and need much attention, affection, and stimulation from their parents. Some ardent nursers still want the comfort of the breast several times a day, but most, if they are otherwise engaged, don't think to nurse unless they get hurt, are very tired, or are sick. This doesn't mean nursing isn't still important to them, but it no longer plays such a prominent role in their lives.

If you wean at this age, you will be primarily helping your child find other ways to get the emotional satisfaction she finds in breastfeeding. Substitution of other activities, distraction techniques, and changing parts of the daily routine work best. Going slowly, watching your child for signs of distress, and giving your child plenty of attention and support will make the transition easier. If your child is nursing more than you like or has some nursing habits that annoy you, you both may be happier if you work on changing those situations rather than attempting total weaning.

Some children will wean easily at this age with a little encouragement, and others will wean on their own before turning three. It is not a measure of your child's maturity if she does or doesn't wean before age three. Each mother's and child's needs are different. Some mothers find they no longer enjoy nursing at this age. Other mothers find it a satisfying experience. Still others continue to nurse at this age mainly because they know it is important to their child.

it is not a measure of your child's maturity if she does or doesn't wean at a certain age.

Three-Year-Olds

Three-year-olds may have a number of favorite activities they prefer over nursing, and most find waiting to nurse much easier than they used to. Many only nurse to sleep and upon waking, while others still enjoy a few other nursing sessions each day. Some three-year-olds nurse even less than once a day.

Weaning at age three involves both substituting other activities and negotiating limits on nursing. It becomes easier to keep nursing private at this age, especially if you have been using a nickname or code word for breastfeeding and have discussed with your child where she may or may not nurse. Many three-year-olds are naturally often busy with other activities. When they're bored, they may ask to nurse just to get a busy mother's attention. Many mothers on the path to natural weaning take the "don't offer, don't refuse" approach at this stage, even though they aren't planning on quitting nursing completely. This means allowing the child to nurse when he requests it but not offering to nurse him at other times.

As at any other age, weaning at age three works best when it's gradual, and the child needs to continue to feel your love and support in many ways during this time. At age three, the end of the breastfeeding relationship is often in sight. Susan Redge of Michigan says this about her nursing three-year-old:

The most important thing I have learned from La Leche League is to meet my child's needs. As a baby, he needed to be held close and nursed often. As he has grown, his needs have changed. He needs to know I am there for him, and at age three there are still times when nothing else but nursing can calm him. It has many times turned a kicking, screaming, out-of-control toddler into a calm, smiling, confident, and contented young man, bravely ready to face his world.

Now he's been telling me that only babies nurse, and he is a big boy. He mentions various friends who don't nurse. Sometimes he even falls asleep without being nursed. I can believe that I probably will not have a nursing four-year-old. I just hope I can satisfy his needs then and beyond as easily and with as much joy.

Four, Five, and Older

Children beyond the age of three do not usually nurse regularly, though it is sometimes still the favored way to go to sleep. Many children wean on their own during this time. Weaning that happens past the age of three years is not necessarily any more "natural" than weanings that occur earlier. A natural weaning is a weaning that happens on your child's individual timetable, when her needs for nursing are fulfilled.

With older children, weaning can often be encouraged by talking about it and coming up with a plan, such as resolving to wean on a birthday. Being straightforward in discussing nursing and weaning can be quite useful at this age. It's important to state your point of view clearly and simply, but it is equally important to listen to what your child has to say on this subject. By this age, your relationship with your child will be rich with many types of shared activities: cooking together, reading aloud, throwing balls, playing pretend games, singing, cuddling, back rubs, and talking. These are all good substitutes for nursing, and most mothers find that they have slowly been replacing nursing with these activities without realizing it.

Older nursing children may still be passionate about their love of nursing, and can often talk about it quite eloquently. Diane Wiessinger of New York writes about how important nursing was to her son as an older child:

Eric's legs grew longer and still he loved to nurse, although we rarely nursed during the day anymore. He would march downstairs to me at bedtime, pajama feet flapping, and announce, "I'm here for the official 'iss' (nursing)." But now I found those bedtime nursings increasingly annoying. I still loved nursing Eric in the abstract, and I didn't look forward to losing it, but I usually resented the reality of the little boy who took so long to fall asleep. I read or counted or twisted my hair, and wished I could get away. We tried nursing in the afternoon instead of at night, but the bedtime nursing was just too important to him. Gradually, there came some nights when he forgot to ask. Sometimes I could talk him out of it by promising to read an extra book. Finally, Eric was nursing only several times a month, at most, and only after I put up some resistance. Nursing was no longer freely given. Big brother Scott took Eric's part from the next bed. "Oh, Mommy, I think it's silly for him to still want to nurse, but if he wants to nurse, why not let him?" I would follow that wisdom for awhile, and then I would start dragging my heels again. Nursing a five-year-old did seem a little silly.

One summer afternoon, Eric and I drifted idly around our pond on floats. Out of the blue, he said wistfully, "You know, Mommy, sometimes I like to think about my favorite things. Like ducks. And nursing. But sometimes when I think about my favorite things, then I don't have them anymore."

"Oh, Eric," I said, "does nursing mean that much to you?"

"Yes," he answered, in a sad, little voice.

"Well then, you shall have it."

"Even when I'm thirteen?" he asked, perking up.

I laughed. "Well, I don't think you'll want to when you're thirteen, but yes, even when you're thirteen."

I was sure he'd want to nurse that night. He didn't. I don't think he nursed for another week or so, but now he knew for certain that he could. The pressure was officially off. Soon we started to go weeks or even months between nursings, and those nursings were rarely more than a minute or two long. My sense of irritation was replaced with curiosity. How long does the unpressured child nurse? Do they ever really quit?

Eric is nine now. He dresses like a ninja, regales us with bathroom humor, and loves dirt bikes. A year ago, while he was cuddled in my lap (because even ninjas need to cuddle), he asked to nurse. I tried to joke with him about it; it seemed absolutely absurd (not to mention acutely embarrassing) to nurse an aging second-grader. But he was really quite serious and persistent.

I fumbled with my shirt and stalled for time, wondering wildly what kind of psychological damage occurs in this culture when an eight-year-old nurses. Something mercifully distracted him, and the moment passed. The next morning, Eric had a whopping case of chicken pox. He hasn't asked since then.

For all practical purposes, I suppose Eric weaned at about five or six, but it's not an issue that we have discussed since that day in the pond. Our agreement was that the door would always be open if he really needed it. I sometimes wonder if, years from now, a tall, bearded bank president will walk through my door with a special request for a little old lady.

chapter 5 • gently encouraging weaning

There are times when a mother needs or wants to encourage weaning. She may be pregnant, or for other reasons she may feel it's time for her child to wean. Even mothers who are following the natural weaning process sometimes find their children need some encouragement to let go of nursing, or to cut back on the frequency as they get older. Liz Koch from California says this about encouraging weaning: "My kids loved nursing. They would have never stopped. I was the leader—kind, but definitely the leader."

This chapter is designed to give you many ideas and possibilities for encouraging weaning. It won't give you a magic formula for weaning or even a step-by-step guide. Children are highly individual, and one standard approach to weaning isn't likely to bring a positive outcome in most children. Thinking about your child's needs, preferences, and abilities can help you decide on an individualized approach to weaning. Part of making weaning gentle and positive is tailoring the weaning process to your child.

Signs a Child May Be Ready to Wean

Children offer clues to their developmental needs all the time. A baby reaches for things, and parents offer safe and interesting objects for him to grab and hold. A toddler insists "I do it myself" and parents let him, whenever possible, practice his skills in dressing or serving himself a scoop of applesauce. In the same way, a child's behavior may contain clues that he might be ready to wean or ready to lessen his dependence on nursing.

> The following list is not intended as a "test" of weaning readiness, but as a guide to understanding your particular child. Some children will show many signs that they are ready to wean, but still cling to a few crucial nursing sessions. In others, steady progress toward weaning will accompany the appearance of more and more signs of readiness. These signs are just common-sense clues that your child is lessening his dependence on nursing and you are finding new ways to meet his needs.

Some signs your child may be ready to wean are:

a child's behavior may contain clues that he might be ready to wean.

Your child is at least one year old.

Your child has been gradually showing less interest in nursing.

Your child is eating a variety of good foods.

Your child is secure in his relationship with you.

Your child has begun to accept other ways of being comforted besides nursing. (For example, when your child falls and hurts his knee he doesn't always ask to nurse.)

Your child can be reasoned with (at least part of the time) about not nursing at certain times or in certain places.

Your child sometimes falls asleep or goes back to sleep without nursing.

Your child shows little anxiety when gently encouraged not to nurse.

Your child, when offered a choice, prefers to play, read, or do something else with you rather than nurse.

Considering all these factors will help you determine how important breastfeeding is to your child's sense of well-being. Weaning happens easily when your child's need for emotional sustenance through breastfeeding has been fulfilled and he no longer relies on breastfeeding as he once did to help him feel calm and secure.

Deciding on a Strategy for Weaning

When encouraging weaning, there are many factors that influence your progress. You will need to be flexible. If your child isn't showing many of the signs of readiness in the preceding list, you will know that weaning may not happen easily. Giving your child as much time as possible, and being patient and understanding, will be important.

Gently encouraging weaning takes much time and energy. Your child will need additional support and attention from you to compensate for less nursing. As Liz Koch of California recognizes, "A mother sometimes has to substitute an hour of sitting and playing for a couple of minutes of nursing." Getting help around the house, streamlining your life for a while, and preparing simpler meals will help you find more time to spend with your child. Encouraging weaning can be a lot of work, but most mothers find they can get through this stage when they are certain that this is what they want to do. If you are feeling ambivalent, uncertain, or guilty, you may find the job of encouraging your child to wean more demanding and difficult.

Don't feel as though you have to stick to your weaning strategy one hundred percent. In some situations, the wisest thing to do is to give in and nurse. A child who is hurt and upset, has a bad cold or the flu, or is just plain desperate can be allowed to nurse without having this episode thwart your weaning plans. Being flexible and responding to your child's needs is just as important during weaning as during the time when you met your child's needs freely at the breast.

Even though you are encouraging weaning, don't expect it to happen quickly. Many mothers report that it takes anywhere from two or three months to a year to wean completely. In some cases, when the child is ready to wean and only needs a little encouragement, weaning happens quickly. But usually, a child's attachment to nursing decreases slowly. Take one day at a time. Children change rapidly, but not necessarily on our timetable. You may not see daily progress. By allowing enough time to take weaning slowly, you and you child can make the adjustments necessary to end your breastfeeding relationship positively and smoothly.

Techniques to Gently Encourage Weaning

There are many ways to encourage a child to wean. Read through the suggestions that follow, and decide which ones are most likely to work for your child. Some of the techniques won't appeal to you or your child. Some you may feel sure won't work in your family. Some techniques succeed even when you don't expect they will work at all. Try only one or two of these techniques at a time. Don't overwhelm and confuse your child by trying too many things at once.

These techniques are primarily intended for children past one year of age, and some of them are only appropriate for children past two, or even older. Obviously, you won't have a rational two-way conversation about weaning with a fourteen-month-old. But this might be a good approach for a child over three.

Don't offer, don't refuse

The idea behind this technique is that mother stops suggesting that the child nurse, but still nurses at the child's request. In some situations with a frequently nursing toddler, this technique doesn't change things much. In other cases, this is a major step toward weaning. Jane Abramowitz of Israel writes about how this technique helped her to wean when she became pregnant while nursing her three-year-old:

First of all, I decided to "wean" myself. This was not as easy as it sounded at first. I decided to cut out every nursing where I asked her if she wanted to nurse. Believe it or not, that cut out at least half of her ten nursings day and night. But it was difficult. I exhausted myself carrying her around and comforting her or simply keeping her quiet and out of the way during homework time or television programs. I spoke a lot less on the phone, read a lot less, and simply sat and did nothing a lot less, and for a couple of weeks life was very hard. She, let me emphasize, was perfectly content. I never once told her she could not nurse when she asked to, I only stopped initiating any nursings for my comfort. I also refused my husband's request to "nurse her for ten minutes so I can eat in peace," as well as my older children's requests to "let her nurse, will you? She's bothering us again; we can't play our game."

Jane's daughter began to enjoy a greater variety of activities and to spend less time clinging to her mother. She was happy and content through it all and weaned easily.

"Don't offer, don't refuse" is a common way to begin encouraging a child to wean. The technique doesn't require putting difficult limits on the child. This is also a good technique to use in combination with some of the following ideas. Many mothers find they naturally start to utilize this strategy when a child gets older. Mary Pierce of New York offers an additional thought on "Don't offer, don't refuse":

I often think that the maxim "Don't offer, don't refuse" should be followed with the phrase "unless desperate!" I usually think this when I say to my frantic, hysterical, so-crabby-and-tired-he's-forgotten-about-nursing child, "Let's have some 'beep-bees,' honey." I also think of it on "twelve-beep-bee" days as I stand in the kitchen, still in my nightclothes at 2:00 PM, with dirty dishes up to the ceiling and no plates to eat from and beg my son, "Wait, just a little while, please!"

Distractions and substitutions

This is a popular way to encourage weaning, and when handled gently and positively, distraction is a natural way to encourage weaning. Weaning is, after all, substituting one thing for another. Some toddlers actually prefer the substitute to nursing, while others are adamant that nothing is an adequate substitute and cannot be distracted from their desire to nurse. Here are some popular substitutions and distractions.

Food and drink. Many toddlers will nurse less if they are not hungry or thirsty. Offer snacks and water, and remember to offer them before the child asks to nurse. Sometimes a toddler will accept a snack if you suggest it when he asks to nurse, but if the child protests. you will probably go ahead and nurse anyway. Keep your child's favorite nutritious snacks on hand: grapes, apple slices, popsicles made from fruit juice, pureed fruit and yogurt, whole grain pretzels and crackers, etc. Cutting food with cookie cutters, making little pizzas with vegetable faces, and other tricks may make snacks more appealing to a toddler. Carry snacks with you on errands and trips, and keep a bottle of water with you when you leave home. It can be tempting to offer candy and sweets to a toddler to distract him from nursing, but you might want to consider if this is really a good idea. With plenty of healthful snacks in the refrigerator or the diaper bag, you won't be tempted to buy less nutritious snacks on your outings.

Reading and books. According to the surveys for this book, reading stories with children is a popular step in weaning. Often we begin reading to a child long before we intend to wean, and story time slowly replaces nursing as the child gets older. Linda Crispell Aronson, in her book, *Big Spirits, Little Bodies,* says books are an ideal substitute for nursing: "Books are just an extension of the breast. After the breast comes books.... [Reading aloud] can bond parent and child, calm and comfort, and shift the child into a state of slumber. It can be a time of great intimacy, free of distraction or intrusion."

Using books to encourage weaning might mean reading with your child as a way to give him the extra attention he needs. Suggest a story before he asks to nurse, or as a regular part of the daily routine. Read a book in bed in the morning before getting up, or after lunch as a prelude to a nap.

Involve children in your daily chores. Toddlers enjoy doing work. When they're happily occupied working near you, they are less likely to ask to nurse. They like to do what you do—wipe off the refrigerator with a cloth, pour the measured cup of flour in the bowl and stir, open the junk mail, play with a sinkful of warm water with plastic and metal dishes. Granted, working with your child takes more time and is messier than doing the job

when handled gently and positively, distraction is a natural way to encourage weaning.

alone, but it can also be viewed as an enjoyable time together, with the chance for you to get chores done as a bonus.

Be prepared with fun activities. Many toddlers are just as happy to do an engrossing project as they are to nurse, especially if they aren't tired or overwhelmed. Keep on hand some homemade playdough, paints, crayons, and other craft items that are developmentally appropriate for your child. If you are worried about the possible mess, you can allow your toddler to create in his high chair, on a table outdoors, or in the basement. Puzzles, games, and toys that encourage using imagination can also be helpful. These activities are most helpful if you suspect your toddler often nurses from boredom. Some children will be so absorbed they will play quite happily alone while you do other things. For other children, special toys and activities for weaning won't work well unless you play and create along with them.

Total, focused attention from mother. If you suspect your toddler often nurses just to connect with you, you may want to try this technique. Make sure there are plenty of times a day when you look at your toddler, listen to him, play with him, and drop what you're doing to respond to him. Is nursing the only surefire way your child has for getting your attention? If you find yourself saying "no" to requests to play or read or go outside, but you always say "yes" to nursing, you may be encouraging your child to nurse simply because it is the one sure way he has to get some quality time with you. Practice responding warmly, quickly, and reliably to other requests from your child. If the child you're trying to wean has a younger sibling, try using the baby's naptimes as special one-on-one times with the older child.

Invite other children over to play. This works best when your child is showing signs of enjoying interaction with other children. One other child is usually enough, and playing with this friend will occupy your child so thoroughly that he doesn't think to nurse. In some cases, an older child or a teenager who enjoys playing with small children might make the best playmate. Keep the time appropriate to your child's attention span and patience—an overwhelmed child is likely to want to retreat to mother to nurse! Stay nearby, in the background, so your child can play without worrying whether you're still there.

Get out more. Many children don't think to nurse when they're away from home. They are so intrigued by their surroundings they don't want to stop exploring to nurse. Take your child with you to the store, on errands, and also to fun places like local parks, museums, and the zoo. Even a hardware store or the mall is interesting to toddlers. If you keep your list of errands short and allow plenty of time for your child to explore, you can have a pleasant excursion together. Take walks, either with both of you walking or bring the stroller. Take bike rides with your child in a bike seat on your bike. Go hiking in the woods, visit the library. An added benefit of spending time outside every day is that your toddler may sleep more soundly and not wake as often to nurse at night.

Stay home more. Some sensitive children find going out to be too difficult and end up wanting to nurse more for comfort. If this is true for your child, work at staying home and keeping life comforting and predictable for your child. Have your partner do errands for you, or do them when he can be home with your child.

Find new ways to touch your child. It can be tempting to physically distance yourself from your child if every contact with you makes him think about nursing. But many mothers find the best way to wean is to step up the amount of holding and carrying, especially with a child under two years. Often it works well to carry a child in a backpack instead of near your breasts. Other mothers find the child is happy to substitute touching mama's breast for nursing while going to sleep, or he may put his mouth on the breast but not suck. Hugging, snuggling while reading or watching television or videos, rocking together in a rocking chair, holding hands, rubbing your child's back, and giving your child a massage are all ways to stay physically in touch.

     If your child seems to request nursing with every touch from you, try making physical contact into a raucous game. My toddler and I like to play a game called "Knock Down" where I sit on the bed, knees up, and my child gently knocks me back. We also play a game where I hold her and say "I'm not going to let you go!" Then I loosen my grip and she crawls away while I teasingly object and try to catch her again.

Delaying nursing

Some mothers find they can encourage their child to wean by postponing nursings. This works well with a child who nurses fairly regularly. Postponing a nursing by ten minutes, and postponing it another ten minutes the next day and the next, may eventually turn two nursing sessions into one. Promising to nurse, saying "yes, but later" is a good strategy when your child asks to nurse in a place or at a time when you are not comfortable nursing. During the night, you could pat or rub your child's back a bit before nursing; some children will fall back asleep before they get a chance to nurse, and others will nurse less. You might also get a child to nurse less if you delay nursing until after meals and snacks.

Planning with the child

If your child has a good command of language, you will want to discuss your weaning plans with him. Most likely, this will be a series of small, relaxed conversations over a period of time, perhaps starting with the simple idea that he will want to wean someday. Over the next few weeks your discussions can get more specific. You may find it helpful to read together and talk about the book MAGGIE'S WEANING by Mary Joan Deutschbein (available from La Leche League International). It may be appropriate to read some of the weaning stories in this book to your child as well. You will want to share your feelings about nursing with your child, such as explaining that your nipples are sore due to pregnancy, or that you would like nursing better if you didn't nurse anymore during breakfast. Be sure to put these reasons for not nursing in the form of "I-messages," so that your child is not made to feel responsible for your feelings. ("I want to get up and have breakfast in the morning because I'm hungry," rather than "You nurse for so long in the morning. Couldn't we stop?")

You may want to suggest some ideas for weaning to your child, such as weaning on a birthday, having a party when he weans, offering a reward, or nursing only at bedtime. Ask your child—he may have some good ideas you haven't even considered. Weaning is an important milestone for the older child, and allowing him to make some of the plans and decisions will help him feel more in control and proud of his accomplishment. Be open to the possibility that your child may be unable to actually follow through on his plan, despite his earnest intent.

Involve dad

Many families say the father plays a big role in weaning. Dad can give the child some of the extra attention he needs and provide a distraction from nursing by playing and interacting with the child. During the day, dad might take the child with him when he goes out, or involve the child in his household tasks. Fathers often take over the nighttime routine for a while (or permanently), reading, bathing, and helping the child to fall asleep. During the night, a father can get the child water or rub his back to help him fall asleep in place of nursing. Becky Riancho of Ohio writes about her husband's role with their large family:

Evening nursing was always the last to go so I would have Dad hold and cuddle the toddler to sleep. It worked great. The child weaned plus became very close to his or her dad. He does not have much interaction with the babies until they are ready or I am ready for them to wean, so this has worked very well for us. And it's great for Dad and the babies!

Stay on your feet

This is a tiring technique for mothers, but if you find your child thinks about nursing whenever he sees you sitting down, you can try staying on your feet as much as possible. You can pay bills and do other paperwork standing at the kitchen counter and fold laundry standing at the table. Some toddlers won't ask to nurse if you sit down on the floor and play with them, rather than sitting on the couch or in a rocker. This is a technique that shouldn't be confused with avoiding your child in other ways. Talk to him, meet his eyes, play, and involve him in your tasks whenever possible.

Change routines

Sometimes weaning happens during a change of routine, either by accident or design. A change in routine removes the reminders that "this is a time we nurse" and works best with children who seem to nurse according to routine cues. A new bedtime routine, introduced slowly and maybe involving the child's father, can eliminate a bedtime nursing. If your child sleeps with you, you might want to try moving him to a sleeping bag next to your bed and see if he wakes to nurse less often. (Some mothers find that allowing the child to continue sleeping with them is a good way to offer security during weaning.) Changing routines during the day, for example, getting out of bed before your child wakes in the morning and having a tempting breakfast ready, might prompt the child to nurse less. If your child nurses a lot in the morning, plan to get up and go out together in the morning for errands. If you have a favorite nursing chair, rearrange your furniture and put the chair in an out-of-the way place for a while. Use a naturally occurring change of routine to your advantage, such as a busy, happy time during the holidays or while on vacation. Many mothers report that it's easier to wean in the spring and summer when they can be out in the yard, meet friends at the park, and go to the pool.

Shorten nursings

Making nursing sessions briefer is often acceptable to toddlers, and can be of great help to pregnant mothers whose nipples are tender. You can choose to nurse in a distracting place, such as in the family room where the older kids are playing rather than in a quiet bedroom. Some toddlers will agree to stop nursing when you count to ten, or when a timer rings, or when you have finished singing a song. Some will stop if you say, "Okay, let's play now." At night, you can say you'll nurse for a certain time, then stop and give a back rub until the child falls asleep. You might have success with using a doll or puppet to "talk" to the child and lead him away from nursing and into another activity. Some families give these short nursings a name, such as "little bit." They allow the child little nursings during the day, and save long nursings for bedtime.

Restrict nursing to certain times or places

Limits on where and when a child may nurse are often introduced to keep nursing private, but they can also be a way to introduce weaning. You may

sometimes weaning happens during a change of routine, either by accident or design.

have nursing rules, such as only at home, or only at certain times of the day. Many families have found their children accept the idea of waiting to nurse until the sun is up in the morning. Making these rules as concrete and understandable as you can will help your child comply. He may require some gentle, but firm, reminders from you until he understands you mean what you say.

Offer a reward or weaning party

Many families have reported success with this method, usually offering to give a reward, such as a coveted toy or outing, or have a party when the child hasn't nursed for several days or longer. For some children who are able to set goals and understand them, this can be a good way to wean and leaves the child feeling proud. It can also be used as a gentle ritual to mark the end of nursing.

Some children are able to sacrifice nursing for a few days to get the reward, but aren't yet ready to wean. This can be a disappointing experience for everyone. Children are not experienced enough to be aware of the ramifications of their decision, and may think that they will wean for a party or special toy, but are devastated that they can't nurse anymore when the excitement of the party is over.

Give up

Giving up on trying to get the child to stop nursing may not sound like a weaning technique, but several mothers have reported it worked for them. With some children, the more weaning is encouraged, the more they want to nurse. Sometimes when the mother surrenders to the idea that this child is going to continue nursing, the child weans himself a little while later. In other cases, where the child just isn't ready to wean, giving up on the idea of trying brings mother, child, and the whole family peace and a more relaxed and happy attitude. Some children ask to nurse less when they know they can nurse at any time. This compromise may suit both child and mother.

All of this said, surrendering to the idea of continuing to nurse is not an easy thing to do and is not always an option. Often surrender comes only when a mother feels she has exhausted all possibilities, or when she and her child are so stressed by trying to wean that encouraging weaning no longer makes sense. In any case, giving up on trying to wean right now doesn't mean that you can't resume weaning later, when both of you feel more ready and less worn out.

Weaning Compromises

Some mothers find they don't want to wean completely, but they do want to change some nursing patterns. Or perhaps a mother needs to wean temporarily, but wants to resume nursing as soon as possible. Here are some ways to encourage and support a child in a partial weaning.

Cutting back

Helping a child eliminate several nursings a day without weaning totally can be a good compromise for both mother and child. The child doesn't entirely lose the security and pleasure of nursing, and the mother gains some control and leeway in the relationship. Many mothers long to put an end to nighttime nursings; others want their child to do other things during the day besides nursing repeatedly. Often, when a partial weaning or "spot weaning" is employed, the mother feels more positive about continuing to nurse, and the child is happy to continue to have some of his needs met through nursing.

     Many of the above techniques can be used to eliminate some nursings while continuing others. You might find it easier to wean from some feedings if the ones that remain are special for you and your child. Kathy Myer of Washington writes about this option for her older child when she was tandem nursing:

> *My three-year-old was given "Sacred Nursing Times." These were times she could look forward to that she would not be denied for any reason—delayed maybe, but never denied. During these times I made sure I was positive about nursing, telling her how much I loved her, and how much I liked to cuddle with her.*

Temporary weaning

Sometimes a mother needs to wean temporarily for a medical reason, to take a medication or have surgery. Again, the above techniques can be helpful. To maintain your milk supply, you may also choose to pump during the period when your child is nursing very little or not at all. When you aren't at all ready to wean, this technique can help you and your child feel hopeful and comforted by the reassurance that nursing can resume again as soon as possible. For more information on medical situations and indications for weaning, see Chapter 7, "Pressure to Wean," or call your local La Leche League Leader or lactation professional.

     Kari Carter of Ohio tells about her experience with temporarily weaning her toddler son:

Just after my son, Daniel, turned two, I noticed a large lump in my right breast. A visit to the surgeon confirmed that the mass had to be surgically removed, and the slight possibility that it was malignant meant we had limited time in which to take care of it. "Let's schedule the surgery in three or four weeks," the surgeon suggested, "to give you time to wean him."

I was dumbfounded. Three or four weeks? How was I to coax an extremely strong-willed toddler, in three or four weeks' time, to surrender his most cherished, lifelong pastime? The doctor warned that because the lump was so close to the nipple, milk leakage from the incision site and infection (mastitis) were probable complications if I did not wean Daniel before surgery. Whenever I had previously tried to deny Daniel the breast (when I was tired, in a hurry, felt he should eat more solids, etc.), I had met with the most dogged resistance and heartbroken cries I had ever heard. I had been feeling ready to reduce the number of nursing sessions each day (though Daniel did not agree!), but even I was not ready to end our nursing relationship so abruptly.

I knew that neither the surgeon nor Daniel's pediatrician, who knew little about nursing toddlers, could offer informed suggestions. Calls to my La Leche League Leader and an LLL member who had been in a similar situation brought me a much more acceptable solution: wean Daniel on the affected breast only, and perhaps only temporarily. These were two possibilities I hadn't dreamed of, for I hadn't known that one breast could stop producing milk when the other was still in use, nor did I know that one could wean for a couple of weeks then resume nursing. But I was reassured that even if I weaned Daniel from both breasts during those short three to four weeks, I would still be able to produce milk afterwards. Weaning from the right breast would probably reduce but not necessarily prevent milk leakage from the incision, and it would greatly reduce the possibility of mastitis in the post-surgical healing period. Meanwhile, Daniel could still nurse on the left side before and immediately after my surgery. I could have my surgery and keep Daniel happy, too!

Weaning strong-willed Daniel from even just the right breast proved quite difficult, however. For almost three weeks I tried to do it gradually on my own, covering the right side with a bandage for part of the day, explaining to Daniel that Mommy's breast was "owie," etc., only to meet with relentless screams and pushing. Finally, a little more than a week before the surgery, my husband intervened and calmly explained to Daniel in words I was certain he wouldn't understand that Mommy was going to have surgery, would have an "owie" in her right breast, and needed Daniel to stop nursing on that side. My headstrong toddler suddenly became much more cooperative, requesting only occasionally to nurse from the other breast, using much less physical force, and resigning himself without screaming to not nursing on that side. Five days before my surgery, Daniel was completely weaned from my right breast.

The surgery went well, and thankfully, the lump was not malignant. I was reassured that the sedative used to make me drowsy would wear off quickly, thus not affecting my nursing toddler. Afterwards, when a large elastic bandage covered my entire torso, we did manage to delay Daniel's nursing until after lunch. When he did finally nurse from the left breast, some pain occurred in the right side, but it was far from unbearable. A few days later, in fact, Daniel asked to nurse from the right side, and he did so causing little pain to the almost-healed incision.

I was a little nervous about resuming nursing on the right breast. During the weeks and months following my surgery, I experienced varying but relatively minor pain as the incision healed and scar tissue formed, but thankfully there was no mastitis. Most of the pain came during the let-down or when Daniel latched on too forcefully. At times I asked Daniel to forgo the right side because my "owie" was especially painful. I soon learned which was his favorite side: he'd point to the right side first, saying "No owie!" then point to the left side and proclaim "This side owie!" For many weeks he persisted in trying to convince me that the left breast was the painful one!

It is now two months after my surgery. I no longer experience pain in the right breast though a small lump of scar tissue is still present. Daniel's nursing is back to normal. By following informed suggestions from mothers who had been through similar situations, I was able to avoid complications from surgery without the trauma of abruptly ending a successful breastfeeding partnership. In fact, the temporary weaning posed such a minor interruption to our nursing schedule that I am back to struggling with my pre-surgery mission: to reduce the number of feedings per day!

Stories from Mothers Who Encouraged Weaning

Some of the stories in the chapter on natural weaning show that mothers often encourage weaning to some extent, even if they are allowing the child more or less to set the pace. The following stories come from mothers who were actively encouraging weaning. Jacqueline Cote-Warren of Nova Scotia, Canada tells her story:

I had to wean my daughter after I became pregnant with my son due to a problem with weight loss on my part. (Before my second pregnancy I had to eat six meals a day to maintain my weight.)

I weaned in about a month's time. I started with distraction techniques to get my daughter to cut back on nursing during the day. Then I moved on to stop night nursing. Because Jessica was sleeping with us (still is), many people told me that I would never get her to wean at night. But moving her out of our bed and weaning at the same time would have been too traumatic for her. I talked to Jessica during the day and told her there would be no "na nas" at night (meaning from the time I went to bed until the sun came up).

The first night with no "na-nas," Jessica woke up and started trying to nurse. I said, "There are no 'na-nas' at night, Jessica." She started to cry while I cuddled her and offered her a drink of water. She took the drink but still cried a little. Just when I thought that it was too hard for her, she fell asleep. All in all she cried only five minutes. The next night she woke up and asked again. I again offered the water. This time she had a drink and went back to sleep. After that she would wake up and say, "It's dark: no 'na-nas,'" and go back to sleep.

After night weaning was well established, I made a real effort to cut back on daytime nursing. Jessica didn't want to nurse if she was busy (especially outside our home), so we kept quite busy. During this time I had to teach Jessica how to cuddle with me without nursing. I would say, "Snuggle me like you snuggle Daddy."

We got down to two nursings a day, and then we seemed to hit a wall. I couldn't figure out how to end these last two nursing times and make weaning final in a gentle and loving way. Finally I said to Jessica, "Now that you are a big girl and don't need 'na-nas' anymore, is there a special treat you would like?"

I figured she'd ask for a doll or some other toy but instead she said, "A party, a birthday party." I explained that it wouldn't be a birthday party, but we could have a party.

The next day I invited three children and their mothers, and we had a weaning party. I made cupcakes, and we played games and had a great time. Jessica was thrilled.

About two days after the party Jessica asked to nurse. I said, "Jessica, don't you remember? We had a party."

And she said, "I'm a big girl. I had cupcakes." That was the last time she asked to nurse. She was totally weaned and we were both happy. I know that she was doing okay emotionally because during this time she also toilet-trained herself. Children don't tend to learn new skills if they are under stress.

May Ripma of California felt it was time to wean, and explains how she encouraged her daughter to do so:

Lee fell down and scraped her knee tonight. I picked her up and held her, we cleaned the scrape, bandaged it, and then swung together on the porch swing with her head on my shoulder. After a few minutes she noticed that the bush behind us was in bloom and off she ran to pick a few flowers. Then I realized that through it all she had never asked to nurse. Tomorrow is Sunday, one week since the last day we nursed, and I know she is forever weaned.

Our weaning fell somewhere between natural and planned. Lee is twenty-seven months old, but was still nursing three times a day until three weeks ago. At that time for a number of reasons, I developed cracked nipples. My nipples healed quickly, but the situation left me with strong feelings that I was ready for weaning.

I had envisioned a completely natural weaning, hoping that Lee would give up nursing on her own. But I had to admit that our nursing was a two-way relationship and for several reasons I was ready to stop.

The first day I told Lee that my nipples were sore and asked her to wait to nurse until naptime the next day. She obligingly agreed, and then, even after I told her my nipples were better, we continued to nurse only once a day for about ten days. Although she asked to nurse a few other times, she was easily distracted. Because she gave it up so easily, I knew the time was right for weaning.

Then last Sunday, during a family camping trip, Papa Mark and I found a quiet moment to talk with her. We talked about when she was a baby and how she couldn't talk to ask for help or comfort, how she couldn't eat by herself, or play with her toys, or do any of the things that she could do now instead of nursing. And because she was big enough now, we wanted to ask her to stop nursing. I told her that she could nurse one more time at naptime that day but that would be the last time.

When I asked her whether she did want to nurse that one last time, she emphatically said "Yes." And she did nurse for a long time with obvious pleasure before she fell asleep.

She really only asked to nurse once more, the next day at naptime. I very gently talked with her, repeating our conversation of the previous day. She cheered up almost immediately and began to talk with enthusiasm about how very big she was getting to be and how she was going to grow even bigger. I am happy with our weaning, and I can tell Lee is, too.

Lisa Campbell of Texas encouraged weaning when she became pregnant:

I became pregnant when Justin was thirteen months old. The first trimester was difficult, with painful, sore nipples. But I was undecided about when, how, and if I wanted to wean him. Here's what helped me: support from my husband and sister-in-law, reading, deciding I would wean slowly, deep breathing before Justin began to nurse, and good alternatives to nursing at naptime and bedtime—holding, singing, and lying in bed together. It worked! Justin is now eighteen months old and nurses only in the morning. I hope to have him weaned soon. I feel the need to prepare psychologically and physically for the next child.

Barbara L. Foster of Ohio also encouraged weaning during pregnancy:

I became pregnant when my daughter was twenty months old. Here are some of the things that encouraged her to wean.

When she crawled into bed for our morning nursing, I would get up and go to the bathroom (something made necessary by pregnancy) before nursing her. Upon my return she would usually be asleep.

We dispensed with a nursing at naptime by eliminating the nap, which she rarely needed. When she needed a nap, a ride in the stroller or car usually got her to sleep.

At night, our daughter usually nursed to sleep in our bed, but we made a new rule: if she went to sleep in our bed, no "nummies," but she could nurse if she went to sleep in her bed. She usually chose to sleep in our bed.

Because of breast tenderness, I would tell her that she would have to stop nursing if Mommy was hurting. I would endure as long as possible before telling her I hurt. She was able to regulate the frequency and I could control the duration of the nursings.

Although there was a new baby on the way, my daughter was sometimes still a baby herself, and I allowed her to nurse when she definitely needed to.

The stories above illustrate families who found positive, creative ways to encourage their children to wean. Encouraging weaning, when done with love and respect for the child, can be a positive step forward.

References

Aronson, L. C. *Big Spirits, Little Bodies.* Virginia Beach, VA: A. R. E. Press, 1995, 78.

chapter 6 • some perspectives on natural weaning

Michelle is having her first baby, and her friends and family were eager to give her a baby shower. Crowded in her sister's living room amidst the pastel-wrapped packages are a variety of women: co-workers from Michelle's office, Michelle's sister-in-law who is single, her sisters who have five children between them, her mother, two aunts, and her grandmother.

"Are you going to breastfeed?" asks one of the aunts.

"I will, if it works out," Michelle replies timidly.

"Yeah, well, just don't do it forever like my neighbor does," says the single sister-in-law, Adrienne. "She still nurses them when they're walking!"

"I nursed my babies back in the sixties when almost no one else did," says the other aunt. "I weaned them when they were four months or so."

Michelle saw her sister roll her eyes. "You should nurse until they're a year. That's what I did with mine. And they don't need it after that."

"It's not a big deal how long," chimes in her other sister. "I weaned Charlie when I went back to work."

"My doctor said I didn't have enough milk," Michelle's mother said. "I wished I had been able to nurse you girls longer."

Regina, a woman in her late forties from Michelle's office, softly spoke up. "I was one of those who nursed my babies even after they were walking and talking. I'm glad I did, but I got a lot of flack from my family about it."

"I nursed all my babies," Michelle's grandmother said. "We lived on a farm so far from town, and we were poor, so it was the only way. But my sisters who lived in the city thought I was pretty backward for doing it."

Michelle was listening carefully, hoping for some useful advice but feeling more confused than ever. So many opinions! So many ways to go! How would she ever know what to do?

Different people hold many different ideas about weaning. This chapter will look at some of these beliefs. Understanding what advice-givers may think and feel about weaning will help you sort through your own feelings and beliefs.

What the Medical Community Says

Health professionals in the United States are pretty much in agreement about how to wean a baby from the breast: gradually, by slowly withdrawing one feeding at a time. But there are differences in opinions about when a child should be weaned, whether extended nursing is beneficial, and if natural weaning is important or even possible.

The World Health Organization (WHO) and the United Nations Children's Fund (UNICEF) both recommend at least two years of breastfeeding. The current recommendation of the American Academy of Pediatrics is "that breastfeeding continue for at least 12 months, and thereafter for as long as mutually desired." However, many doctors advise mothers to wean during the first year or by the baby's first birthday. Even doctors who are supportive of mothers breastfeeding a young baby or who are flexible about other behaviors, such as toilet learning, may still believe that babies should be weaned at a predetermined time. But not all doctors take this view.

Many child care experts have a "mom and baby know best" attitude toward weaning. Penelope Leach writes in *Your Baby and Child: From Birth to Age Five:*

Only you and your baby can decide on the right time to start weaning. A few babies get bored with breastfeeding and take to a cup even before their mothers feel ready to start stopping. A few mothers see no reason to wean their babies at all. They go on breastfeeding until the baby is a toddler who is using the breast entirely for comfort. As long as it feels right to you and your baby, either extreme or anything in between is fine.

Other physicians share her view, including Dr. Virginia Pomeranz in *The First Five Years:* "When should a mother stop nursing? As with most aspects of child raising, this is a very individual matter. I would say that she should nurse as long as both she and the baby enjoy it."

Often doctors support later weaning, but with some reservations. In *Touchpoints: Your Child's Emotional and Behavioral Development,* T. Berry Brazelton writes about weaning an eighteen-month-old:

> *The only reason I'd urge weaning would be if it were interfering with her becoming independent. But if she is autonomous in all other domains, the closeness is all to the good. . . . A reunion at the breast is so lovely after a working day or after a day of negativism and turmoil.*

Dr. Benjamin Spock believed that breastfeeding for nine to twelve months is adequate for "complete breastfeeding," but thought it was fine to nurse up to age two if baby and mother so desire.

Other doctors advocate weaning based on child readiness, and see many benefits in a long nursing relationship. Dr. Marianne Neifert, in her book *Dr. Mom's Guide to Breastfeeding,* writes:

> *What starts out as principally a method of feeding a newborn gradually evolves into principally a method of comforting and reassuring an increasingly independent toddler or preschooler. Baby-led weaning guarantees that the process is paced according to the child's unique dependency needs rather than society's expectations or the mother's preference.*

Dr. William Sears, who advocates natural weaning, speaks similarly:

> *Don't limit your breastfeeding to a predetermined length of time. Follow your baby's cues. Life is a series of weanings, from the womb, from the breast, from home to school, from school to work. When a child is pushed into one of these steps before he is ready, he is at risk for less-than-ideal emotional development.*

Dr. George Wootan, writing in his book, *Take Charge of Your Child's Health: A Complete Guide to Recognizing Symptoms and Treating Minor Illnesses at Home,* also recognizes that the child "should determine when he wants to wean. Unfortunately, this does not often happen in our culture. For a variety of reasons, we tend to wean our children before they are ready, and I fear we overlook the needs of the child in doing so."

And many doctors echo Dr. Antonia Novello, former Surgeon General of the United States, who said, "It's the lucky baby, I feel, who continues to nurse until he's two."

What Mothers Say

While physicians are often considered the experts on breastfeeding by many people today, it wasn't always that way. Turning to physicians for breastfeeding information and advice is a relatively new practice. It wasn't until the late 1800s that doctors were consulted on matters of infant feeding. For the majority of mothers before that time the "experts" were other mothers.

Other than the child, the mother is the person most intimately involved in the weaning process. Mothers relate many different weaning experiences, and have many different feelings about weaning. Some mothers feel serene and confident, while other mothers feel confused, impatient, or uncertain. (Many mothers feel one way part of the time, and have completely opposite feelings at other times.) The weaning stories in this book show the variety in mothers' experiences.

While each mother has her own personal reactions and stories related to weaning, mothers also have much in common. Women have weaning wisdom to share and often can give another mother information and support not available from physicians. This wisdom is the basis of much of the information La Leche League provides, and the underpinning of this book. Mothers' stories and experiences in weaning can be very helpful to other mothers, giving support and strategies that are practical and time-tested.

Mothers who choose a planned weaning may be doing so because they are pregnant, tandem nursing, have a health problem, or feel that it is time to wean. Each mother has her own idea about how long nursing can or should go on. Ann Davis of Ohio tells about when she felt ready to wean:

When my first two children weaned, it was because I actively encouraged them to do so. It was a period that I do not recall clearly, for it stretched over a long period of time, and their nursing is much more memorable than their weaning. Both nursed well into their preschool years, Sean until he was three and Jess until she was four. It is perhaps somewhat tongue-in-cheek to say that I found nursing them at that stage a much more draining experience than they did, but it is entirely accurate in all senses of the word. I was ready to quit long before they were. Their desire for the closeness and comfort of the nursing experience was so strong. At the point at which I encouraged them to wean, I was tapped out, and I was starting to feel that nursing was no longer an enjoyable experience for me. Perhaps I was giving into cultural pressures of what should be expected of children at their ages, but I began to look at my children differently as they grew older. It became harder to accept that these children, no longer babies or even toddlers, still needed to nurse. Their abilities and

mothers' stories and experiences in weaning can be very helpful to other mothers.

appearances changed how I thought about them, and I found it necessary for me to treat them differently, to develop a new relationship with the new parts of their person and their new abilities, a relationship that didn't include a ready access to nursing for comfort or going to sleep.

Mothers who have chosen to wean naturally or gradually often choose to do so because of the way they understand their child's needs. The vantage point from which they view their child's growth and development helps them understand the role of breastfeeding in their child's world. Following are some ways that mothers have put natural weaning or weaning gradually into perspective.

Look to the baby

Mothers often say they have learned about weaning by looking to their babies for understanding. One mother from Massachusetts wrote that "weaning is not about logic or charts or time. Weaning is about readiness. I only know this because I can see that my baby is not ready to wean. She hasn't shown me at all that she is ready to wean, and she is the one person whose opinion on this subject counts." When a mother looks to her child, she often sees how important nursing is to the child, and sees the hole that would be left if she weaned prematurely. For many mothers, this is the main reason they continue to nurse. When mothers initiate weaning, they continue to look to their child to understand which weaning techniques are most appropriate for them.

Time will tell

Many mothers speak about being patient and waiting for weaning to happen in its own time, rather than imposing a deadline. Often mothers don't come to this understanding overnight but grow into it. Shelagh Pruni of Ohio writes, "As my first son grew from a newborn and throughout his first year, I learned—first by following my heart, second from La Leche League—how important and special nursing was to him and decided to let him wean when he was ready." Not needing to have a scheduled date for weaning is mentioned by some mothers as a liberating experience. Other mothers choose to break time into small chunks and decide to continue to nurse another week or another month or until the child's next birthday before they consider weaning again. Mothers who decide to begin weaning also take their time, trusting that a gradual, patient approach is best for baby and mother.

Continuing to nurse past one year has many advantages. Mothers say breastfeeding is helpful with many of the new challenges they face as their baby turns into a toddler. Gloria Finkel of Pennsylvania found that nursing helped with challenges even beyond the toddler stage.

My son Jacob nursed until shortly before his fifth birthday. Toward the end it was only once a day (at night before he went to sleep), but even so, it was important to him, and I found it an invaluable tool for making mothering easier. The year Jacob was three was more challenging than when he was two. I couldn't imagine weaning him then! It would have been traumatic for both of us. I see mothers trying to calm and comfort their children with bottles, blankets, stuffed animals, but for Jacob, nursing always worked like magic.

Mothers also comment on the personal benefits they received from sharing a long nursing experience with their child. Debbie Weiss of Arizona writes:"Breastfeeding him has given me a great boost in my confidence as a mother and the deepest feelings of love I have ever known."

Weaning is a positive step forward. Weaning wisdom from mothers shows they often see weaning not as an end, but as a new beginning. Jennifer Hayes, from North Carolina, notes, "Weaning has felt like one more step in her transition from totally dependent infant to toddler explorer to child discoverer."

What Fathers Say

Fathers and mothers often have different perspectives on breastfeeding and weaning. In the book *Mothering and Fathering,* Tine Thevenin explains that typically fathers are concerned with helping their children toward independence, while mothers are interested in making the relationship with their child close and connected. So while a mother may see the nursing relationship as a way to connect with her child, a father may see it as a hindrance to independence.

Larry and Susan Kaseman, of Wisconsin, offer another idea on how fathers may view later weaning:

Appreciation for long-term nursing can be even more challenging for a father. Not only does he not experience the physical closeness, emotional satisfaction, and hormonal benefits of nursing that a mother does, he may also feel left out of the nursing relationship and have trouble supporting what seems to him to be a drain on his wife's drive and physical resources.

Fathers may also frown on continued breastfeeding because they want to be alone with their wives more often, or they went to be able to go away overnight with their wives and think weaning will make this easier. Some fathers would like to be more involved in their child's life and feel that the mother's continuing to nurse the child excludes them.

Many fathers are supportive of their wives' decisions to begin weaning and become actively involved in the weaning process. They take over at bedtime, help establish new rituals, and spend more time with their child. Sometimes they even help to initiate weaning. Mike Adams from Pennsylvania writes:

When Daniel was approaching three, he continued to talk about his sincere desire to nurse for a long time. I didn't think his nursing would ever end, but my wife was determined to let Daniel lead in his decision to wean.

One day, I suggested to Daniel that one week after he had weaned we would have a weaning party for him. Daniel pondered it for a while and decided on a date to wean. True to his word, he stopped nursing on that date, and a week later we had a weaning party. Since he stopped nursing Daniel has not even hinted at wanting to nurse again.

After all of this, I have to admit that there was a little sadness in my heart when Daniel finally weaned. I guess he is growing up faster than I want him to.

Many fathers, given the time and respect from their wives to arrive at their own conclusions, begin to see the importance of breastfeeding played out in their family life. Just as mothers find their opinions on weaning change as their babies grow, the same happens with many fathers. Bridgett Sanders from Illinois writes, "My husband, Steve, was supportive of nursing, but how long to nurse was another matter. He thought that a couple of months would be enough. But now after nine months with no end in sight, he has gotten more relaxed about it. Weaning isn't even mentioned anymore."

Kathy Richardson of New York noticed her husband was affected by observing their daughter.

When Sam was in her fifth year, Gary made his one and only comment related to weaning. Sam had nursed to sleep—it took about ten seconds in those days. Gary walked into the room and stood looking at us lying on the bed. "She's awfully old to be nursing." He paused, and I cringed at the thought of what was coming next. He continued, "But she looks so peaceful for the first time today." And he turned and walked away.

What Children Say

Babies express their appreciation for breastfeeding with their body language. Any mother who has nursed at least a few months has experienced her baby eagerly anticipating a feeding while she hurries to untuck her shirt and undo her bra. Babies often relax quite suddenly once they've begun to nurse, or stop nursing for a moment to smile up at their mothers.

Babies who continue to nurse into toddlerhood may express their attachment to nursing verbally. Sitting on my lap, my two-and-a-half-year-old daughter said, "'Me-me' makes me feel good," and then settled down to nurse. The son of Adele McHenry from Michigan declared, "Mommy milk makes my tears go away." Toddlers often comment about the good taste and warmth of their mother's milk, and the affection they feel for their mothers who supply this. It's not uncommon for a toddler under stress to express an urgent need to nurse by shouting, "Nursey now!"

A nursing toddler's earliest jokes are often related to breastfeeding. Linda Hewitt of Pennsylvania tells how her daughter expressed her love for nursing in a unique way: "She said she wished she could remove my breasts and carry them around with her!"

Diane Weissinger's son, Eric, called nursing "iss-iss."

I would ask him, "Eric, would you like to read a book?" (This to a toddler busy at my breast.)

He would grin, pull away, and shake his head. "Iss-iss," he'd say.

"Would you like to go dancing?"

"Iss-iss."

"Would you like to take a walk?"

"Iss-iss."

My daughter thinks it's funny when I ask her if she wants to "me-me on the roof" or "me-me on the sink." Our other joke is related to what breast milk tastes like. I ask, "Does it taste like apple juice?" and she laughs, "No, milk!" When I asked my son similar questions, he liked to tease me in return by saying, "No, it tastes like ice cream! It tastes like spaghetti!"

Children often speak about weaning as well. Sometimes they'll ask questions that reveal they are contemplating the subject. The daughter of Cynthia Wick of Michigan asked, "Grown-ups don't need nummy, do they Mommy?" Some children become very interested in whether other children they know still nurse.

Once they have weaned, they may say very little about it. Missy Parkinson from Tennessee says when her daughter weaned, "Nothing was actually said and she never looked back." Others announce the news of their last nursing like Alice Ziring's son from Washington who said, "I don't need 'mama' to go to sleep anymore." Charlotte Lee Carnhill's son, Colin, proclaimed that he had weaned by saying, "No more nursing, Mommy. Me big now." Rosemary Gordon of New Zealand recalls that her son surprised her by opening her nightdress, then closing it and saying "No, I don't want it anymore" and never nursing again.

Some children seem quite proud of their accomplishment, like Clara Acosta's daughter, of Colombia, who said, "I don't nurse anymore, because I'm a big girl now, but if ever I feel like a little girl I know I can have 'me-me.'" She was obviously happy to have that little escape hatch! Many children see weaning as a sign of their growth. Margaret Stevick of North Carolina says that after she weaned, her daughter would sometimes do something she couldn't do before and say, "Look, I can do this now, I'm weaned!"

Children may continue to mention nursing, even after an otherwise untroubled weaning. Carol Narigon of Ohio says that even though her daughter, Sophie, has been weaned more than a year, "during times of stress she wishes she could have 'ummies.' She remembers the safety and comfort she felt and misses the taste." Donna Seifert of Illinois says that when her son, Jamon, had been weaned for a year and a half, he said, "You know, Mom, when I was a baby and I nursed, I liked it."

What Anthropologists Say

Determining what is a natural weaning age for human beings raises some problems. Human beings' ideas about when and how to wean are often determined by culture, not necessarily by what is best or natural for babies and mothers. Anthropologists who have studied weaning have found a great variety in weaning ages, from birth (in much of the United States and Western society in general) to age seven or eight in other cultures. C. S. Ford, in a 1945 study of sixty-four non-industrialized societies, found the usual weaning age to be about three to four years, adding, "Weaning seems to be delayed as long as it is at all possible in the great majority of our primitive societies."

Katherine Dettwyler, PhD, from the Department of Anthropology at Texas A&M University, has determined that the average world weaning age is about 2.8 years, but also notes:

 It is meaningless, statistically, to speak of an average age of weaning worldwide, as so many children never nurse at all, or their mothers give up in the first few days, or at six weeks when they go back to work. It is true that there are still many societies in the world where children are routinely breastfed until the age of four or five years or older, and even in the United States, some children are nursed for this long or longer. In societies where children are allowed to nurse "as long as they want" they usually self-wean, with no arguments or emotional trauma, between three and four years of age.

human beings' ideas about when and how to wean are often determined by culture.

Dr. Dettwyler has used the example of primates to try to determine a natural weaning age for humans, since "gorillas and chimpanzees share more than ninety-eight percent of their genes with humans" but are lacking the cultural biases of humans. By comparing a variety of factors, including when permanent molars appear, length of gestation, size of adults in relation to other mammals, age when sexual maturity is reached, and size of the primate when weaned, her research suggested that a natural weaning age in humans would be a minimum of two-and-a-half years up to a maximum of seven years.

In Western society, for much of recorded history, there has been a tendency to put great stock in the age of weaning. Dr. Marianne Neifert recognizes the fallacy in this point of view: "Weaning can be quite a controversial subject in our culture. In other cultures weaning is a natural event occurring on its own like the eruption of teeth or the first steps. This more casual attitude toward weaning will serve you and your baby well."

Western society has long valued accomplishment in the public arena and at the same time devalued the importance of home and family and women's contributions there. For a long time women were kept out of the public sphere entirely. Now that women have gained a more prominent place for themselves in business, politics, and other areas, there is still a tendency to see motherhood as a disadvantage and obstacle to success in more important arenas. This may explain why this same society has many cultural restrictions related to breastfeeding and weaning. Anthropologists have noted that societies that value motherhood and women's biological functions are often the same societies that encourage mothers to keep their babies close and not to wean them for several years.

Customs in Western society have made breastfeeding a more difficult feat than it need be. Socializing is typically done without children in tow, industrialized jobs and office work are not well suited to children being present, and nature is in general mistrusted or seen as something that people manipulate to their advantage. Firmness in parenting is applauded, and meeting the needs of babies and small children is often seen as being indulgent.

Primitive societies with later weaning ages also have times for adults to socialize, and mothers in these societies do work, but children are present most of the time, and when the mother is busy, an older child or adult is often nearby to help with the baby. Natural processes are often more respected as well, and babies' needs are seen as something that parents naturally respond to. In the book *Childhood,* author Melvin Konner tells about reading a passage to a ¡Kung woman from Dr. Benjamin Spock about the importance of having schedules and ignoring the baby's cries while you work about the house. Dr. Konner explains the mother's reaction: "The ¡Kung mother looked bemused and disapproving. 'Doesn't he understand he's only a baby, and that's why he cries?' she said. 'You pick him up and comfort him. Later, when he grows older, he will have sense, and he won't cry anymore.'" Dr. Konner adds, "The ¡Kung bet on maturation—and they have never yet had a child who didn't outgrow crying."

Anthropologists have noted some correlation between nonviolent, cooperative societies and later, gentler weanings. But all societies are made of fallible human beings. There is no perfect society and no perfect model. Looking to your baby and to your own heart is a far better way to determine what is best for both of you.

Historically Speaking

What have breastfeeding and weaning customs been like in the past? Margaret Ehrenberg, writing in *Women in Prehistory,* says more than ninety percent of the people who have ever lived on earth were foragers or gatherers. The typical weaning age in forager societies, then and now, is about four years. Many experts speculate that weaning occurred earlier once agricultural societies developed, maybe due to the availability of grains more suitable for weaning food.

Written accounts of weaning ages exist from periods throughout Western history. Stories in the Bible suggest that three to four years of age was a common time to wean. The Talmud encourages mothers to nurse until eighteen months to two years. Two years of nursing is recommended in the Koran. Customs in ancient India suggested that longer nursing increased longevity.

Valerie Fildes, author of *Breasts, Bottles, and Babies: A History of Infant Feeding,* has looked at breastfeeding and weaning patterns throughout history. She notes that there is evidence of an average weaning age of three in ancient Egypt and Babylon. Most likely weaning took place at one to two years in medieval Europe and during the Renaissance. Weaning was often determined by customs related to the season of the year or the phase of the moon, and boys, sickly children, and twins were often nursed longer.

Fildes found that early weaning and supplementary feeding can be traced back as far as the Ancient Greeks and Romans. Both cultures may have weaned infants as early as six months, introducing solids early. While weaning between the ages of one and two years was typical in medieval Europe, women who were wealthy enough employed wet nurses and usually didn't breastfeed at all. Fildes believes that throughout Western history, weaning was often accomplished suddenly and with no concern for the child's feelings. The child would be suddenly separated from her wet nurse, or weaned overnight by the mother. The mother would sometimes apply something bitter-tasting to her breasts. Interestingly, experts who wrote about weaning often encouraged gradual weaning. In many cases, common weaning foods were poorly suited to the nutritional needs of weaned babies.

Rima D. Apple, in *Mothers and Medicine: A Social History of Infant Feeding 1890-1950,* explains how Western mothers shifted from breastfeeding and wet nursing to feeding primarily with homemade or commercial substitutes for mother's milk. This practice began in earnest in the late 1800s as a way to prevent infant deaths in babies who were not able to breastfeed. Eventually, bottle-feeding became a recommended practice for all babies. Breast milk substitutes were promoted by doctors, manufacturers of infant foods, and by the social customs of the period. Substitutes for breastfeeding were deemed to be "just as good as the breast" and increasingly breastfeeding was viewed as fraught with difficulties. Also, more and more mothers were giving birth in hospitals, and hospital practices made it difficult for mothers to breastfeed successfully. Wet-nursing fell out of favor as well at this time.

With increasing reliance on technology in the early twentieth century, women lost faith in their ability to breastfeed, and relied on the medical establishment instead of their mothers and friends for breastfeeding advice. Those mothers who did breastfeed were encouraged to give supplemental bottles, in part because it would make weaning to a bottle at an early age easier. Consequently, during this time, many mothers never breastfed, and those who did often weaned within the first days or weeks following birth.

Breastfeeding rates in the United Sates reached an all-time low in the early 1970s, but soon there was a resurgence of interest in breastfeeding. The culture's newfound faith in the wisdom of nature along with research into the immunological properties of human milk led to an increasing awareness among mothers and doctors that "breast is best."

Though much traditional wisdom about breastfeeding had been lost during decades of bottle-feeding, La Leche League and the natural childbirth movement had rediscovered how to breastfeed successfully during the 1950s and 1960s. Women who were motivated to breastfeed found the information and mother-to-mother support they needed in these organizations. However, many of these mothers continued to wean iafter only a few months of breastfeeding. The percentage of children breastfed past the age of one remains quite small, influenced by many factors including mothers returning to work and the belief that children should be independent and self-reliant at an early age.

Learning the history of weaning can illuminate the culture around us, but our decisions about weaning are far more personal than historical.

Globally Speaking

In much of the world today, weaning does not occur until at least two years of age. In Kenya, twenty-five percent or more of the babies are nursed past three, and some children nurse as late as eight. In Malaysia, mothers typically nurse several years until their babies are ready to wean. The forager societies that still exist, such as the ¡Kung and Mbuti people, practice nursing until about three years. A study of breastfeeding and weaning in the tropics and subtropics by Derrick and Patrice Jelliffe in 1978 showed that the typical weaning age was two to three years in North Sudan, Morocco, Algeria, and India. In Pakistan, ninety-two percent of mothers nurse two or more years. Valerie Fildes studied a number of rural communities in Africa and found the average age of weaning to be about two years.

Many mothers in Western cultures have found comfort and understanding from knowing people who were raised in other cultures because they see later weaning as normal and often were themselves weaned later. When I was nursing my first toddler, I met a young mother from El Salvador, a refugee on her way to a new life in Canada. She saw my two-year-old nursing and was so excited. Using her bare-bones English, she communicated with enthusiasm that she had nursed until she was three and her baby, now eight months, would nurse just as long or longer. Other women I have met from Central America, particularly those who lived in rural communities, have told me how they nursed through toddlerhood, and it comforted me to see how matter-of-fact they were about meeting a toddler's need to nurse. This attitude is echoed by Dr. Naomi Baumslag who says, "In many parts of the world, a woman would be considered guilty of neglect for weaning a child less than two years old."

Knowing that other parts of the world traditionally choose later weaning may or may not impact your feelings about nursing in the society in which you live. Far more important is to decide what is best for your baby and yourself.

References

American Academy of Pediatrics Work Group on Breastfeeding. Breastfeeding and the use of human milk. *Pediatrics* 1997;100:1035-39.

Apple, R. D. *Mothers and Medicine: A Social History of Infant Feeding 1850-1950.* Madison: University of Wisconsin Press, 1987.

Baumslag, N. and Michels, D. L. *Milk, Money, and Madness: The Culture and Politics of Breastfeeding.* Westport, CT: Bergin and Garvey, 1995.

Brazelton, T. Berry. *Touchpoints: Your Child's Emotional and Behavioral Development.* New York: Addison Wesley, 1992, 170.

Dettwyler, K. A time to wean. In *Breastfeeding: Biocultural Perspectives,* ed. P. Stuart-Macadam and K. A. Dettwyler. New York: Aldine De Gruyter, 1995, 39-73.

Ehrenberg, M. *Women in Prehistory.* Norman: University of Oklahoma Press, 1989, 50, 60, 89.

Fildes, V. A. *Breasts, Bottles, and Babies.* Edinburgh: Edinburgh University Press, 1986.

Ford, C. S. *A Comparative Study of Human Reproduction.* Yale University Publications in Anthropology, No. 32. New Haven, CT: Human Relations Area Files Press, 1964, 79.

Jelliffe, D. B. and Jelliffe, E. F. P. *Infant Nutrition in the Subtropics and Tropics.* Geneva, Switzerland: WHO Monograph No. 29, 1978.

Konner, M. *Childhood.* Boston: Little, Brown, 1991, 112.

Leach, P. *Your Baby and Child: From Birth to Age Five.* New York: Alfred A. Knopf, 1990, 195.

Neifert, M. E. *Dr. Mom's Guide to Breastfeeding.* New York: Plume, 1998.

Novello, A. You can eat healthy and enjoy it. *Parade Magazine,* November 11, 1990.

Pomeranz, V. E. with D. Schultz. *The First Five Years.* New York: St. Martin's Press, 1984, 17.

Spock, B. and Rothenberg, M. B. *Dr. Spock's Baby and Child Care.* New York: Penguin Books, 1992, 154.

Thevenin, T. *Mothering and Fathering: The Gender Differences in Child Rearing.* Garden City Park, NY: Avery, 1993, 59.

Wootan, G. with S. Verney. *Take Charge of Your Child's Health: A Guide to Recognizing Symptoms and Treating Minor Illnesses at Home.* New York: Crown Publications Inc., 1992, 121.

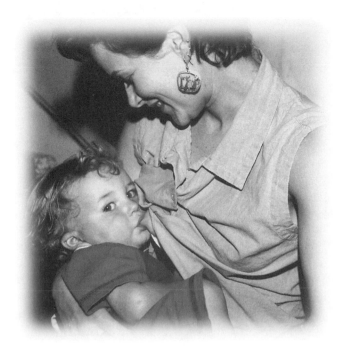

chapter 7 • pressure to wean

Most mothers who are nursing a toddler or a preschooler are very aware that what they are doing is unusual, at least in Western culture. Friends and family members may make this very clear, with support from pediatricians and other parenting "experts." Mothers are surrounded by social signals that pressure them to wean early and to push their children to be emotionally independent. Messages from all of these sources can make it difficult for a mother to listen to her own heart and intuition about her nursing child's needs. This chapter explores the many ways in which mothers feel pressured to wean before their children are ready and offers suggestions for dealing with criticism about extended nursing.

Social and Cultural Pressure to Wean

In the USA, seventy-four percent of mothers who are breastfeeding wean by the time the baby is six months old. Yet the American Academy of Pediatrics recommends nursing "for at least twelve months, and thereafter for as long as mutually desired." Research shows there are many benefits for children and mothers who practice extended nursing. (See Chapter 2, "What Natural Weaning Is Like.") And many mothers who have tried extended nursing have found it to be both positive and beneficial. What causes weaning to happen at an early age? And why do so many people believe that nursing should not continue into toddlerhood and beyond?

Factors that contribute to premature weaning

There are many reasons for early weaning, but the most important one is how breastfeeding is managed. Factors that lead to premature weaning are: introducing solids early (before the middle of the first year), not continuing to offer the breast as the primary food source in the first year, using pacifiers frequently, and offering supplementary bottles of food other than human milk. Following a three- to four-hour feeding schedule rather than nursing in response to the baby's cues also contributes to early weaning. Sometimes weaning happens around one year of age because of the naturally occurring distractibility of the nine- to fourteen-month-old. Finally, when mother or baby are often separated, there is also a greater likelihood that weaning will happen prematurely.

Other major contributors to premature weaning are cultural. In "Beauty and the Breast," an article in *Breastfeeding: Biocultural Perspectives,* anthropologist Katherine Dettwyler explains how cultures can cause mothers to wean early. By promoting breastfeeding mainly as nutrition for infants, seeing breasts only in a sexual light, and not accepting nursing in public, a culture can encourage mothers to wean early. Also, if a mother doesn't encounter other women who are nursing older children, she is not likely to consider the possibility of nursing longer than the women she does know.

Yet even in cultures that aren't supportive of breastfeeding, some mothers do practice later weaning. How do these mothers end up breastfeeding for a longer time? A study by K. M. Buckley published in the *Journal of Perinatal Education* identified three distinctive behavior patterns in mothers whose babies nursed longer:

> *A healthy dependence of the child on the mother*
>
> *A close physical relationship between mother and child*
>
> *Sharing of sleep arrangements.*

These mothers saw nursing as an important aspect of their relationship with their child and said it seemed as though it was "the natural thing to do." They were also most likely to have practiced nursing their babies on cue and for comfort, and not to have offered supplements too early. La Leche League's book THE WOMANLY ART OF BREASTFEEDING says, "You are certainly not out to set a record for prolonged nursing. Late nursing is not something you strive for, but it is a very special relationship between you and your child."

Myths about extended nursing and late weaning

Many people know little about extended nursing beyond myths and old wives' tales that have no basis in fact or in research into child development. Yet these beliefs are often repeated from one mother to another, from mother-in-law to daughter-in-law, or even from physician to patient. It's important to recognize that beliefs about extended breastfeeding are often distorted by other culturally based ideas about children, parenting, and even sexuality. Taking a closer look at some of these oft-stated theories of weaning can sometimes put to rest a mother's doubts about her own extended nursing and weaning experience. Recognizing these myths for what they are will also help you deal with criticism from others.

A child will never wean on his own. If you haven't experienced a natural weaning, you might think a child couldn't possibly wean on his own. This might be especially hard to believe if your child is very attached to nursing right now. But children grow and change dramatically in the first several years of life, and their interest in nursing changes as they do. Children want to nurse only as long as it fills a need for them. Sometimes this need will last for several years, sometimes far less. As Dr. William Sears points out in NIGHTTIME PARENTING, "The main issue is not when your child leaves your bed, but how he leaves. If you don't set a deadline, you won't have unfulfilled expectations. Remember, a need that is filled does go away. It may last a little longer than we expect, but eventually it will pass." This wisdom applies to weaning from the breast as well as learning to sleep alone.

A child who is still nursing is too dependent. It's easy to see why people who aren't familiar with nursing toddlers see them as dependent. If nursing is seen as something only babies do, then a toddler who is still nursing will look as if he is clinging to infancy and the total dependency of babyhood. Yet, in many ways, toddlers still are babies. They may be walking and talking and learning about the world in many ways, but they are also quite unable to provide for their own physical and emotional needs. They have many needs that linger on from babyhood: to cuddle with their mothers, to be comforted when they're hurt, frustrated, or confused, and to have help easing into sleep. These needs are all naturally met through nursing, and it is a wise mother who recognizes and honors her child's need to be dependent. Trusting the child in this way builds the self-confidence needed for later independence.

Nursing toddlers often exhibit a very sturdy independence in areas unrelated to breastfeeding. My daughter, at two-and-a-half, wants to "do it myself!" She has learned to buckle her sandals, but very slowly. What I could do in thirty seconds takes her a determined ten minutes or more.

children grow and change dramatically in the first several years of life and their interest in nursing changes, too.

This is the same little girl who asks to nurse when she's tired or has had enough of the challenges of her world. Some might see her independence about her sandals and her love of nursing as contradictory, but I believe they go hand in hand. She gets some of the inner strength she needs to be independent from the time she spends on my lap having "me-me." Many mothers find that nursing doesn't inhibit their child's independence, but helps to foster it.

Extended nursing is a sign of sexual problems. This is a common fear in Western cultures where extended breastfeeding is not the norm. In a culture where breasts are seen as primarily sexual objects, an older child nursing might be perceived by some people as an erotic act. Sexual feelings are not usually a part of the nursing relationship, though some mothers report feeling aroused on occasion while nursing. This is probably because of the hormone oxytocin, which is released during breastfeeding, triggering the milk let-down. Women also experience the effects of oxytocin during lovemaking and during childbirth. Oxytocin has been called the "hormone of love" because of its role in interpersonal acts.

Normal, spontaneous feelings of arousal during feedings may be disturbing to mothers concerned about sexual boundaries. In American culture sexual impulses are often portrayed as uncontrollable, like a heavy truck careening down a hill with no brakes. But this is largely a myth. Adults can control their impulses, whether they are sexual or not. Rather than worry, it is far more helpful for a mother to accept sexual feelings during nursing as a complex, but normal, part of being a woman. One mother, who had been upset about the sexual feelings she was experiencing while nursing, eventually came to a different understanding:

I didn't realize it was guilty feelings I was experiencing with Jason's nursing. I simply didn't like what I felt. I was actually denying myself some really beautiful feelings there. I find, however, that it still takes mental effort to dispose of those guilt feelings and probably will for some time. I hope my children will not have to be performing mental gymnastics to enjoy normal, natural bodily feelings when they grow up!

A related fear is that children who nurse for a long time, particularly boys, will grow up to be homosexual. However, there is no evidence for this. As with many other issues, it is important to remember that extended nursing is the norm for the human species and that the early weaning so common in Western culture is a relatively new practice. There is no evidence that homosexuality is more common in societies that practice later weaning. Children who nurse for several years do not appear to be affected in any way in their sexual development. They may actually grow up to be more comfortable with their bodies and with relationships.

An older nursing child won't learn "self-comforting skills." The ability to meet one's own needs is highly valued in many modern cultures. Babies and young children are often expected to have these skills long before they are really ready to depend only on themselves. In her book *Mothering and Fathering,* Tine Thevenin observes that "in our individualistic society, we expect children to learn at a very early age to get nourishment from another source than the breast, and to find comfort in something other than a human being—pacifiers, teddy bears, blankets." The natural model of extended nursing suggests that these expectations may be inappropriate. Nancy Penny of Texas writes about the beauty of human comfort:

"Of course I weaned my baby," the mother told me. "I had already nursed him for a full five months longer than my first two sons. Now that he is eating solid food, he doesn't need me anymore. The last thing I want to be is a human pacifier!"

The first thing that flashed through my mind when she said this was the odd way our society has recognized the artificial pacifier as the normal object and the mother's breast as the substitute. In advertisements, baby-shower gifts, and store displays, pacifiers are promoted as necessary items of infancy.

Thinking further about pacifiers and motherhood, I considered just what it is that pacifies, that "brings peace." I thought of calm in a storm, or the renewal of sleep, of the bridging of cultures. When a child is crying, she is asking for peace in her young life in the only way she knows, from the mother who is uniquely able to provide it. Learning to give and receive peace in this way equips the mother and child to face anxiety and conflict later, long after an artificial pacifier is discarded. Do I want to be a human pacifier? Now that I think about it, I am sure I do. When all is said and done, that's the best kind.

Giving your child the comfort of breastfeeding is actually the best way to teach self-comforting skills in the long run. It is from this early relationship with you that he learns much about his needs and how to get them met in constructive, self-initiated ways. Filling your child's "baby" needs at the appropriate time in his life will help him understand his own needs and what to do about them when he is older.

A mother who nurses an older child is doing it to fill some need in herself. Mothers who have actually nursed an older child know that children who are still nursing at four are far more likely than their mothers to be the ones actively pursuing nursing. While nursing is a way for the mother to feel connected to her child, and there are still health benefits and practical benefits, few mothers would still be nursing if their child had been willing to wean.

Many mothers explain that their satisfaction and pleasure in nursing declines as the child gets older, and if they continue to nurse, it is primarily because it is important to their child. Older children are not usually coerced to nurse, they are allowed to nurse. Mothers say they do very little to encourage the breastfeeding relationship with an older child other than to let the child nurse when he indicates he'd like to. Barbara Kennedy of New York adds:

 One thing is certain, a baby, especially an older one, is anything but shy about refusing to nurse if he is not interested. There's no way to make an unwilling baby nurse. He will turn you down cold and not care two cents about your feelings in the matter. Knowing this should be reassuring to the mother who is fearful that nursing could be prolonged beyond what is good for the baby because of her own needs.

many mothers find that nursing is the one way they are able to rest.

Prolonged nursing is too fatiguing for a mother. Some people assume that breastfeeding is physiologically stressful. Yet no research supports this idea. In fact, one recent study even suggests that adjustments in the nervous system in nursing mothers make it easier to manage stress. Mothers of toddlers, nursing or not, are often tired. Chasing after a toddler, keeping him safe, and providing for all of his needs require a lot of energy. Many mothers find that nursing is the one way they are able to rest, since nursing assures that there are a few times in every day when the mother can put her feet up and relax with her child. A child who is still nursing is also less likely to be sick due to the immunological benefits of human milk, saving mother from the extra energy it takes to care for a sick child. Children who are still nursing often fall asleep easily at the breast when they are tired, saving parents from the difficulties of prolonged bedtime routines.

The longer you wait to wean, the harder it will be. There is no "critical age" for weaning, but it is true that weaning is easier at some ages than at others. Some young babies will easily accept weaning to bottles, but in many cases infants who have had weeks of consistent nursing will not readily take substitutes for mother's breast. Some mothers choose to wean when their baby is at the highly distractible age of nine to fourteen months, but there are many babies who would not wean easily at this age. And not weaning at nine to fourteen months doesn't mean you are signing on to nurse your child until he is four. Chapter 4, "Breastfeeding and Weaning as Your Baby Grows," may help you to better understand what weaning is like at different ages. As children get older, encouraging weaning often gets easier, not harder, since older children have a greater ability to reason and a wider repertoire of interests. And finally, when your child is ready to wean, it will be easy.

It's better to wean suddenly and get it over with. Some people still suggest it is best to wean quickly and to cut off that aspect of your relationship with your baby or child almost overnight. One common way to wean quickly is to leave the child with someone else for a few days, while the mother goes on a trip. This is a technique that has been employed throughout history, and even in some cultures where extended nursing is widespread, sudden weaning by separation is advocated. There are many reasons to question this practice however. A small child is not likely to understand why the comfort and closeness he depended on is no longer available to him and is likely to feel deserted and pushed away. Also, sudden weaning is difficult for the mother. It can lead to problems with engorgement, plugged ducts, and breast infections. Emotionally, the mother may feel distressed or sad. This is partially due to sudden hormonal changes. Lactating women have higher blood levels of prolactin, the milk-making hormone which is also associated with feelings of well-being. When a mother weans abruptly, the drop in prolactin is sudden as well. This can be particularly difficult for a mother already prone to depression.

Another approach to sudden weaning that is common but not recommended is the "spicy mama" technique, which involves putting something like hot pepper sauce or some other foul-tasting substance on the nipples. The theory is that the child will be disturbed and upset by the bad taste and refuse to nurse after that. (In reality, he may very well want to nurse despite the taste.) Hot pepper substances contain oils that can cause pain on the sensitive skin of the mother's areola and the child's mouth and lips, and even less noxious substances can cause unwanted side-effects in you or your child. This alone suggests that the "spicy mama" approach is best avoided. Also, weaning in this manner can leave a child feeling tricked or confused.

A third approach to sudden weaning is to use stories or other methods to frighten a child out of nursing. This also is not a good idea. While talking about weaning can be helpful once your child has a good grasp of language, telling stories designed to scare him will cause confusion and undue fear. Your child will benefit far more from an honest discussion on his level about weaning, where you share your feelings and expectations in a simple way he can understand.

While the above approaches are swift and to the point, they are not advisable. Sudden weaning is not good for babies or nursing children. Suzie Hemphill, from California, writes about the problems that resulted when she abruptly weaned her daughter, Krista:

When my daughter, Krista, was almost three years old, I decided to wean her. It was by far the worst decision I ever made. Krista was very challenging. But our nursing relationship would soothe her and seemed to keep her grounded. She was only nursing at night to go to

sleep and once or twice in the middle of the night. I felt that she was too old to nurse. I thought it was too much trouble to nurse her and that it would be easier if she weaned. I cut her off cold turkey. She screamed and cried for hours for several nights. After that, she would wake up every night several times crying. She would say things like "I'm so sad that I can't nurse" and "My heart is broken because I can't have nummies." My heart was broken, too, but I continued with this program. Krista had been entirely potty-trained, including at night, for three months; she immediately regressed when I weaned her. She began taking a bottle at night so I was changing her diaper five to six times per night. She began having nightmares. This was definitely not easier than nursing!

It's been five months since that awful time that I weaned her so abruptly, and she is just now starting to potty-train again; she still takes a bottle (just one in the middle of the night now); she still has nightmares.

Weaning is one of the many areas in your relationship with your child where going slowly pays off in the long term. There are no instant fixes for people little or big that don't have a cost. By weaning gradually and employing gentle techniques designed to comfort and build strength in your child, you will maintain your child's inner security and trust in you.

Criticism and Pressure from Friends and Family

Many mothers find it difficult to deal with pressure to wean when it comes from family members and friends. When a mother is being told by others that she should wean, she may feel that her needs and her baby's needs are not being taken seriously or that no one understands her breastfeeding relationship with her child in the same way she does. She may also doubt herself and her understanding of her child. Choosing to do things differently than other people calls for a great deal of courage, strength, and self-assurance, as well as a good support system.

Pressure from your partner to wean

When criticism of continued breastfeeding comes from your partner, the person who lives with you and shares responsibility for your children, it can be hard to know how to handle the situation. Fathers urge weaning for different reasons. Sometimes they have clear-cut goals, such as being able to go out with you alone, or to go away for a weekend. It may be that the baby's father longs to be a more important person in his child's life. Sometimes fathers are reacting to fears, often unspoken ones: "Is my son becoming a 'mama's boy'?" "Is my child always going to have first claim to my wife's body?" "Doesn't all this breastfeeding wear my wife out?" "Won't my child turn out weird if she's weaned so much later than children in the other families we know?"

Disagreements about weaning can become a source of tension between parents. If each person holds tenaciously to his or her own opinion and is unwilling to listen to the other's concerns and needs, the impasse that results may point to other difficulties in the relationship. In most cases, though, when both partners are committed to loving and understanding each other, disagreements over weaning can be worked out. Taking time to share feelings and fears can help each parent understand the other, though it may take several conversations over a period of time to come to a comfortable agreement. Listening thoughtfully to your partner's concerns and not discounting his anxieties (even if you don't share them yourself) is very important. You may point out how continued nursing is beneficial to your baby, and how it makes life easier as a family, too. Allow yourself to be open to negotiate. "I'd like to nurse another two months, and then we can talk about weaning again," one mother told her husband.

Sometimes negotiation involves finding creative ways to meet your partner's needs as well as yours and your baby's. If your partner wants you to wean so you can have more time together, talk about how you can make that possible without weaning. Some things other couples have found that work include more hugs and kisses, dates at home once the baby is asleep, renting a video and making popcorn every Friday, taking a bubble bath or shower together. Go away for a weekend with your baby, maybe to a state park lodge for a refreshing break from daily life, or go camping. Many children are happier with relatives, and if yours aren't local, make your next visit longer and ask them to babysit one night while the two of you go out. Dr. William Sears writes this cautionary note to husbands who want to go away for a weekend with their wives:

For the first year or two, avoid pressuring your wife to "get away alone." Many mothers normally do not feel comfortable leaving their babies for more than a few hours or even for a day at a time until a child is two or three years of age. . . . Pressuring the mother to separate from her child before she is ready is doomed to fail, and your anticipated romantic get-away may be much less romantic than you planned. You will have much more fun if you learn to travel as a threesome. . . . Babies are babies for a very short time.

If your baby's father longs to feel more important to your baby, talk about ways he could become more involved. Many families try to build time with father into the daily routine. Playing with the baby every morning while the mother showers, taking a toddler outside every evening after dinner, or giving baths and reading aloud before bed are just a few of

when both partners are committed to loving and understanding each other, disagreements over weaning can be worked out.

the many things a father can do. If baby "only has eyes for Mom," it may take awhile for him to get used to being alone with father. A gradual transition will help. My daughter started to like going with her father on errands when she was eighteen months old, as long as she was the one leaving me. Some families have found father naturally becomes more involved as the child grows older.

If your partner is still intent on your baby weaning, you might see if your child is willing to trade some nursing time for other activities, as a test of her readiness. If this doesn't go well, it will be obvious to all of you that it's too early to wean. Suzie Hemphill from California says that at this point "You will resent your husband if you do something that your child is not ready for just to please him. But if she seems too old to nurse to your husband, then she will also seem too old to do the things that will take the place of nursing. So why not choose the comforting tool that has worked so well up to this point?" Many fathers learn to prefer the peace and quiet of a happy nursing relationship to the stress and strain of forcing the weaning process.

Pressure to wean from relatives

Pressure to wean can come from people in your extended family who may be genuinely concerned that your child will come to harm if you don't wean immediately. Even when these fears are based on old wives' tales or ignorance, you may not be able to convince them otherwise. Often advice is given because older members of the family think that is their duty. Sometimes there are hurt feelings because you are making choices that are different from those made by the rest of the family. Even if you have never said a critical word about your sister-in-law's parenting, she may see your parenting style as a silent rebuff. When it is your parents' or in-laws' example you are rejecting, the sensitivity may be even greater.

If you are being pressured to wean due to fears or biases your family holds, you may want to educate them about extended nursing. Give the information in small batches, respectfully, and give them a chance to respond. Don't worry if you don't have all the answers, or can't match all of their arguments. Some mothers have found it better to say very little, or simply say, "This is what I plan to do. I'd like your support." One tactic that can help put an end to a power struggle is to admit you don't have all the answers and that there is more than one way to parent. Jill Whelan of Indiana describes her strategy for dealing with critical relatives:

 I explain that I believe all parents have to make choices based on their own family's needs and that the way we have chosen is meeting the needs of our family very well. This tends to end any further discussion or argument unless the person is really looking for information, in which case I'm always happy to explain my choices. No bad feelings

result, since I point out that no two families are alike, which implies that there are a wide variety of ways one can meet a family's needs. Also, I believe it is necessary to respect and try to be nonjudgmental about the parenting styles of my relatives if I want them to feel the same toward me.

Don't set yourself up for criticism by family members. When you are around relatives who object to long-term breastfeeding, seek out privacy when your child wants to nurse. Don't bring up the subject, or if others do, answer with a simple, confident "yes, we're still nursing!" and then change the subject. Humor can be helpful as well. In some situations, it may be better if extended family members don't know you are still nursing.

Relatives may want you to wean so your child can come and stay overnight without you, or even have a longer visit. It may be helpful to point out that even if your child were weaned, he would probably not be ready to sleep away from you for a while. If your child is comfortable staying with relatives for a couple of hours without you present, suggest short visits as an alternative to overnights and weekends. Ultimately, your child's needs and security are more important than a family member having a child to himself.

Many mothers report time works on their side. As the child grows, relatives' fears are displaced with pride in "how well he's turning out." Often the criticism is heaviest with the first child. Eventually, they decide that your child is fine or that this is how you do things and it's not worth the trouble to try to change you.

Agreeing to disagree. Sometimes the conflict over weaning simply cannot be resolved, perhaps because of other problems in the relationship. If you continue to press the issue, expecting total acceptance of your decision, you may cause a deeper rift. It's nice to have wholehearted support from family members, but it isn't always possible. Learning to agree to disagree, and to no longer speak about the subject, may be necessary to preserve the rest of your relationship.

It can be painful when people we love and people who have known us since we were young criticize choices we make as adults. We want their approval and want them to respect us. As Janet App from California writes, "There was no way I was going to win them over to my way of thinking or get their support and agreement, so I had to let go of the idea of wanting or needing their support." Janet found "it was a matter of persistence. When they finally saw that I was going to quietly continue doing what I felt was best, without having to justify myself to them, they stopped asking."

Because family criticism can cause you to doubt you own decisions, you need support from other sources. Talking to friends who have nursed older children, attending La Leche League meetings, or reading books on the subject can be helpful. If your husband is supportive, he can back you up or reassure you when the criticism is hard to take. He may also speak to members of his family on your behalf, and choose to field their criticism himself.

Finally, trust your motherly intuition and your ability to know what's best for your child. This is the way to give yourself the support you need. I felt more confident about natural weaning after I pondered this question: "Is there anything anyone could say that would change my mind and cause me to wean early?" I realized there wasn't, and I have felt less vulnerable to criticism ever since.

trust your motherly intuition and your ability to know what's best for your child.

Pressure to wean from friends and neighbors

Friends and neighbors may also pressure you to wean, or at least offer unsolicited advice. These people in your life don't need to know you are still nursing. You don't have to feel dishonest if you don't reveal all the details of your life to friends and acquaintances, and nursing your toddler is certainly a private decision. Answering humorously or lightly and being confident can deflect criticism. Good friends who care about you will usually be glad to hear why you have made the decision to continue to nurse. Some friends, if they have made different mothering choices than you, may feel uncomfortable or threatened. Learning to de-emphasize your differences and not make comparisons can help you preserve and enjoy your friendship.

Pressure to wean can also come in the form of invitations to adults-only social gatherings. Sometimes it's possible to leave your nursing child for the time it takes to attend a social event, but on other occasions you may wish to stay home for the sake of your child. Some parents have a policy that they attend social functions only if the whole family is invited. Others send dad alone as the family representative. Saying you can't leave a breastfed infant with a babysitter is increasingly acceptable, but eyebrows go up if you refuse to leave a nursing toddler behind. You may want to offer a reason that goes beyond breastfeeding, such as, "He would be very distressed if we left him that long." For very special social occasions, creative solutions can make it possible for you to attend. Cathryn LeMay of Illinois found a way to attend a family wedding without leaving her nursing toddler behind:

 My husband's family is spread out all over the country, and we don't get to see them very often, so when his sister got married and didn't want children at the wedding, we decided to work something out rather than stay home. We hired a teenager who came to our house after school about six times in the two-week period before the wedding. I wanted Jeffrey, fifteen months, to get to know her in a non-

threatening environment while I was right there with them. Bridget was wonderfully creative and patient and continued to entice him to play with her. I sat at my desk working, and he soon figured out that he would have more fun with Bridget!

My husband spoke to the director of the country club where the reception was to be held. She assured him that it would be no problem for Jeffrey and Bridget to play in her office while we were in the nearby banquet room and even promised a plate of food for them.

When we arrived at the country club, Jeffrey was asleep. I was able to get him out of the car and into the office and lay him down on a blanket. When we checked on him about an hour later, he was awake and ready to nurse. The evening progressed pretty smoothly, with Pete and me checking on Jeffrey about every hour. At the end of the evening, with the bride's permission, we brought Jeffrey into the banquet room to show him off. He smiled and flirted with everyone and even gave his grandparents a kiss!

Comments from strangers

When a stranger makes a remark such as "You're nursing a kid that big?" or insinuates that breastfeeding a toddler is somehow disgusting or bizarre, it can feel both surprising and hurtful. Most strangers don't have the power to pressure a mother to wean, but they can make a mother feel uncomfortable or uncertain about her choice. Mothers with nursing toddlers often teach them a code name for nursing like "mama" or "nu-nu" to avoid embarrassing situations such as a three-year-old announcing " I want to nurse!" in the middle of the grocery store. In the United States, many mothers no longer nurse in public once a child is older. Mothers have different degrees of comfort on this issue, and often judge each situation individually as to whether or not to nurse.

Cindy Allen from Florida writes about learning to be confident in a public nursing situation with her eighteen-month-old daughter:

My husband and I were eating at an expensive restaurant (the kind that's high-risk with an eighteen-month-old). Just when our food arrived, Lindsay started to get restless. Although by this time Lindsay rarely nursed in public, this time I was happy to oblige because I knew nursing would keep her quiet and busy. I began to nurse while I ate my dinner. Michael and I talked and ate when suddenly he said, "That lady is really giving you a look."

Apparently, a woman across the room was not happy with the activities at our table and was making a point of showing her disapproval. My husband is usually not one to worry about what people think, but he couldn't help but notice this woman's reaction.

I was just about to look at her but stopped myself. I suddenly realized that I really didn't care what she thought. Waiters and bus boys had been scurrying by, and I had hardly noticed. I had learned to turn off my disapproval radar completely. I was so proud of myself! I even remember how good the enchiladas were!

Weaning in Challenging Situations

When nursing isn't going well

Sometimes a mother considers weaning simply because breastfeeding isn't going well and it's hard to imagine continuing to nurse in these circumstances. People who care about her may suggest with the best of intentions that she should "just give that baby a bottle." In this situation, it's important to remember that there are things about breastfeeding that may take time for both baby and mother to learn, and as in any aspect of your child's development, new stages may bring new challenges.

In the early months, breastfeeding may be accompanied by some common problems: sore nipples, engorgement, breast infections, worries about low milk supply, or a baby who won't readily latch on. These are common experiences for many mothers, and can almost always be solved with accurate information, support, and commitment on the part of the mother. THE WOMANLY ART OF BREASTFEEDING offers more complete and extensive suggestions for dealing with these problems. Contacting a La Leche League Leader or a lactation consultant can also help you work through these challenges.

When problems and discomfort make breastfeeding seem like too much of a chore, it can be tempting to wean. Mothers who persevere and give themselves time to solve problems comment on how grateful they are later that they did not give up. Often they gain new confidence and strength from the experience of solving their problem. And they are glad to continue to give their babies all the benefits of breastfeeding. As Mary Humston of Iowa explained, "I 'stuck it out' and can honestly say I am glad that I did, because now I am experiencing the joys and rewards."

Pressure to wean when returning to work or school

Many mothers think seriously about weaning when they go back to work. It often seems like the simplest choice and one that will be readily understood by others. However, there are numerous options for mothers who want to combine working and breastfeeding. As in many aspects of your life as a mother, creativity and flexibility will help you to find the best solution for you and your baby. Some choices you might consider are:

Leaving work or school on breaks to breastfeed a baby who is being cared for nearby;

Working part-time, flex-time, or from home, or in some other way rearranging your work hours to make breastfeeding easier;

Bringing baby to work or school with you;

Hand-expressing or using a breast pump at work or school, and storing the milk so that it can be given to your baby while you are away;

Delaying or modifying your return to work until your baby is older;

Working shorter hours and letting your baby nurse more frequently when you're together.

Many mothers combine two or more of the above strategies, changing their work schedules, their pumping schedules, or their caregiving arrangements as their baby grows. Rebecca Bartlett of Vermont, whose daughter weaned at five, changed her work schedule as her child got older: "I started working part-time when my daughter was three months old. At eighteen months I went full-time. Nursing helped us maintain our relationship despite work. She was in day care/nursery school near my worksite until she was over three years old, so I could visit her at mid-day."

Many working mothers report how glad they are to be able to nurse their babies after they return home from work. Breastfeeding helps to ease the difficulty of being separated from their babies and helps them to feel closer when they are together. Many mothers are also glad to be able to give their baby something no substitute caregiver can—the good nutrition and comfort of breastfeeding. As Betty J. Gravlin of Missouri reports, "Even though I must work, breastfeeding helps me feel more bonded to my children during the workday. I'm proud that I'm able to give my baby a part of myself while I'm away each day. My pumping sessions are reminders of the two most precious people in my world."

Some mothers find that although they are able to work out the details of pumping and storing their milk, their co-workers are not supportive of their decision to breastfeed. Val Ullman of New Jersey found this situation in her office:

The greatest difficulties with nursing and working for me were the interruptions in my daily work routine and the attitudes of my co-workers and my boss. I eventually became used to the interruptions and planned my day around them.

I faced unkind comments about my commitment to my career, and I have repeatedly been asked when I would be finished with this "nursing nonsense." I have always replied, "When Ali is finished." This is where tenacity comes in. Nursing is right for me and my baby. I need

working mothers report how glad they are to be able to nurse their babies after they return home from work.

to nurse Aliana not only for health concerns but because I am gone for so many hours a day. I miss my baby and this is one thing that I can do that no one else can. It is our time to cuddle and talk. It is our special time, and it affords me the security that I need as a mother.

As more working women nurse their babies, I hope it will become the norm and provisions will be made for us in the work place. Until then, we must support and help each other.

If you experience pressure at work to wean, you may be interested in two studies that have shown that breastfeeding mothers miss fewer workdays and breastfed babies are ill less frequently, even when cared for in group settings. Let your colleagues and supervisors know that they benefit from your commitment to nursing your baby. (See the reference list below for more information.)

If you are planning on returning to work or school soon, you will find helpful information in the book *Nursing Mother, Working Mother* by Gale Pryor and in THE WOMANLY ART OF BREASTFEEDING.

References

American Academy of Pediatrics Work Group on Breastfeeding. Breastfeeding and the use of human milk. *Pediatrics* 1997;100:1035-39.

Barros, F. C. et al. Use of pacifiers associated with decreased breastfeeding duration. *Pediatrics* 1995; 95(4):497-99.

Buckley, K. M. Beliefs and practices related to extended breastfeeding among La Leche League mothers. *J Perinatal Ed* 1992; 1(2):4.

Dettwyler, K. Beauty and the breast. In *Breastfeeding: Biocultural Perspectives,* ed. K. Dettwyler and P. Stuart-Macadam. New York: Aldine De Gruyter, 1995, 174-95.

Jones E. et al. Relationship between infant feeding and exclusion rate from child care because of illness. *J Am Diet Assoc* 1993; 93(7):809-11.

La Leche League International. THE WOMANLY ART OF BREASTFEEDING, 6th rev. ed. Schaumburg, IL: La Leche League International, 1997.

Pryor, Gale. *Nursing Mother, Working Mother.* Boston: Harvard Common Press, 1997.

Reves, R. et al. Child day care increases the risk of clinic visits for acute diarrhea and diarrhea due to rotavirus. *Am J Epidemiol* 1993. 137(1):97-107.

Sears, W. NIGHTTIME PARENTING: HOW TO GET YOUR BABY AND CHILD TO SLEEP. Schaumburg, IL: La Leche League International, 1985, 39.

Sears, W. *Keys to Becoming a Father.* New York: Barron's Educational Series, 1991.

Thevenin, T. *Mothering and Fathering: The Gender Differences in Parenting.* Garden City Park, NY: Avery Publishing Group, 1993, 61.

chapter 8 • weaning because of medical advice

Winnie was surprised to hear her friend break into sobs on the phone.

"And the doctor said I had to wean to take the medication," Nancy cried. "Gina will be so upset!"

Winnie didn't know what to say. She had no idea breastfeeding was so important to Nancy or her baby, Gina.

"I just can't imagine weaning her now," Nancy went on. "Not happily at least. What am I going to do?"

Sometimes medical situations arise that force a mother to think about weaning before she feels that she and her child are ready. Weaning may appear to be the only solution to a very real problem. In other situations, criticism from a health care provider may cause a mother to reconsider the wisdom of continued nursing or natural weaning. These, too, are challenging situations that require thoughtful consideration. There are often alternatives to weaning even in difficult circumstances, and there are many creative ways to handle criticism of continued nursing, even when it comes from a doctor or other professional.

When a health care provider suggests that it's time for a baby to be weaned, the conversation may or may not be directly related to a medical concern. Few medical situations actually require weaning, and a physician's advice to wean a nursing baby or child may be influenced by his or her personal beliefs about breastfeeding. It's important to separate facts from opinion when a doctor suggests or even insists that you stop nursing.

When Your Doctor Suggests Weaning

Comments from physicians about weaning are often an outgrowth of discussion at a well-baby checkup. Sometimes weaning is brought up in connection with an issue that is clearly unrelated to breastfeeding. In this situation, it may help to recognize that the advice is not directly related to your health or your baby's.

Physicians have a wide variety of opinions on breastfeeding. There are physicians who understand and support the idea of nursing until your child outgrows the need. Some physicians, though, hold the same opinions about breastfeeding and weaning as do others in the culture in which they live. They may see breastfeeding as only appropriate for young babies. They may view an older nursing child as coercive or too dependent, or may feel that a mother who continues to nurse is doing so to fulfill her own needs. Some doctors see breastfeeding as only a stopgap until a child is old enough for cow's milk from the carton, or has teeth. Others believe erroneously that a mother's milk no longer has any nutritional value after age one. Doctors may also assume that mothers are only nursing to fulfill an obligation, one they'd like to be released from as soon as possible, or that mothers want permission to wean without feeling guilty. All of these beliefs can influence the advice they offer to the mothers and babies in their care.

Some doctors, in the course of the one-year well-baby checkup will say almost offhandedly, "You should be weaning, now that your baby is one." Others might imply that it's somehow better and healthier for your baby to wean, and may suggest there is little or no benefit to breastfeeding now that your baby is one year or older. While this might appear to be medical advice because it is being given by a physician, it is important to note the context in which it is said. Is the doctor suggesting weaning because of a medical problem in you or your baby? (If so, see the following section, "Weaning in Medical Situations.") If this is not the case, it can be helpful to ask what dangers he or she sees in continuing to nurse, and what documented evidence this is based on. It will also be helpful to let the doctor know that breastfeeding is important to you and your baby, and weaning is not something either of you is considering yet.

It is a relatively new phenomenon for mothers to go to a physician for advice on parenting, and even feeding issues were rarely discussed with doctors until the late 1800s. In NIGHTTIME PARENTING, Dr. William Sears points out that "doctors are trained in the diagnosis and treatment of illnesses, not in parenting styles." For help with rearing their children, mothers turned to their own mothers, relatives, and friends for answers and insights. Some mothers today choose to balance their doctor's advice with information from other sources, such as books, other mothers, La Leche League, and their own intuition.

So how can you communicate with a doctor or other health care provider whose opinions on weaning are very different from yours? Some mothers continue to nurse without telling their doctor; this may be comfortable for them, but it doesn't allow the doctor to learn about normal, healthy children who happen to still be nursing. (Not being honest about weaning could also create problems if you later find yourself in a medical situation where the physician must be informed that your child is nursing.) Other mothers choose to tell their doctor they see no reason to wean now, and ask for their doctor's support. Some mothers prefer to find a more supportive doctor. A few may share information, research, and reading material on later weaning with their physician. Ideally, you and your doctor or other health care provider will find ways to work together to best meet your baby's needs, even if this means the two of you must simply agree to disagree.

Weaning in Medical Situations

Rarely do medical situations require weaning. In most cases, there are alternatives that can be considered in order to preserve the breastfeeding relationship. Many doctors are not aware of how stressful weaning can be if you and your child are not ready, and it will be helpful to share your feelings on this matter. In this process, it is helpful to know how to communicate effectively with your health care provider. Stating clearly that you do not want to wean at this time, and that weaning would be stressful and difficult for you and your baby, will help your health care provider to understand some of your concerns. When a physician or other health care provider suggests or insists that you wean, you need to ask for more information. Some questions you might ask are:

Do I have any other options in this situation? Are there other drugs that would be effective but not interfere with breastfeeding? Are there other ways to do this procedure?

Are there reports in medical literature regarding this drug and breastfeeding?

How will my breastfeeding child be affected in this situation if I choose not to wean?

Can the treatment or procedure be delayed until my child is ready to wean? How long can I wait? How will delaying change the outcome?

What might be the outcome if I elect not to do this at all?

Can this procedure be done on an outpatient basis instead of in the hospital?

If I must wean, can I resume breastfeeding later?

If you are uncomfortable with the advice or information you are given, you may find it helpful to seek a second opinion. You may also choose to research the subject yourself, at your local library, at a medical library, on the Internet, or at another resource center. La Leche League Leaders and lactation consultants have access to medical information related to breastfeeding and will help you to find information to share with your physician. In all cases, it's important to stay involved with your health care provider, to communicate clearly, and to work together to find a solution that is acceptable for all of those involved.

Mother requires medication

It is important that you tell your doctor you are breastfeeding whenever a medication is recommended. In almost all cases, a drug can be found that is compatible with breastfeeding. Although most drugs pass into a breastfeeding mother's milk, the amount is very small, usually about one to two percent of the mother's dose, and is unlikely to affect the baby. There are very few cases reported in the medical literature of a prescribed or an over-the-counter drug harming a nursing baby. With few exceptions (such as radioactive compounds), the baby is nearly always unaffected by medications taken by the mother. If studies show that a drug is not present in mother's milk or that it is known to be safe from a long history of use in nursing mothers, you and your doctor need not worry.

Some doctors routinely suggest weaning when you take any medication, perhaps because they know little about drugs in human milk. They will often reconsider this advice or suggest other options if you communicate your desire to continue nursing. In any discussion of medications and breastfeeding, it's important to point out that weaning will be stressful for both mother and baby and may carry its own risks. The risks of giving a baby formula must be weighed against any risks of continuing to nurse while taking the drug.

Sometimes a doctor suggests weaning because of a personal bias against extended breastfeeding. The questions listed above can help you discuss the situation with your doctor. You need to be able to separate the medical advice from the doctor's personal beliefs.

Some other points to consider in a discussion with your doctor:

If the medication is for a minor ailment or pain, discuss with your doctor whether you need to take it at all. In the case of pain medication, are there other ways you could relieve the pain?

it's important to work together to find a solution that is acceptable for all who are involved.

Often a medication that might be considered potentially harmful to a breastfed newborn will not be a problem for the toddler or older child who is nursing less frequently and eating other foods.

Is it possible that the condition will clear up on its own? Is the medication really necessary?

Is there another drug that can be used? There may not be much information available about the use of a new drug in lactating women. In this situation, an older drug that is known to be safe for breastfeeding babies may be preferred, even if it is somewhat less effective.

If there are concerns about side-effects, could the nursing baby or child be monitored while the mother takes the drug?

Despite the considerations and arguments listed here, you should not take the subject of medications and their effect on breastfeeding too lightly. The current American Academy of Pediatrics policy statement on "Breastfeeding and the Use of Human Milk" cautions:

Although most prescribed and over-the-counter medications are safe for the breastfed infant, there are a few medications mother may need to take that make it necessary to interrupt breastfeeding temporarily. These include radioactive isotopes, antimetabolites, cancer chemo-therapy agents, and a small number of other medications.

It is important to take the possible effects of drugs on breastfeeding seriously. This is a complex topic, with many considerations for your health and your baby's. You need the advice of professionals, preferably health care providers who are knowledgeable about breastfeeding.

Sources of information about drugs and breastfeeding. You may need to consult more than one health care provider to find the information you need about a particular medication and to work out a solution to your problem. You may also need to gather some information yourself. Here are some suggestions.

A knowledgeable pharmacist may have information about a drug or references that you could review with your doctor. Your pediatrician may be more knowledgeable about the effects of medication on a breastfeeding baby than the primary care physician or the specialist who has prescribed the drug for you; you could ask your doctor to talk to your baby's doctor before any decisions are made about weaning.

The American Academy of Pediatrics has published an article called "The transfer of drugs and other chemicals into human milk" that lists specific medications and provides information about their use in breastfeeding women. This article is available in medical libraries (see the reference list at the end of the chapter for more information) and is also reprinted in THE BREASTFEEDING ANSWER BOOK, a resource owned by most La Leche League Leaders. Two other publications that contain specific information about drugs and breastfeeding are: *Drugs in Pregnancy and Lactation,* by Gerald Briggs, Roger Freeman, and Sumner Yaffe, and *Medications and Mother's Milk,* by Thomas Hale. Your local La Leche League Leader will also have access to one or all of these books. They may also be available in your local library or can be ordered from La Leche League International. Information about drugs in human milk is also available on the Internet. Your health care provider or pharmacist may have a copy of *United States Pharmacoepia Dispensing Information: Drug Information for the Health Care Professional,* which contains information on drugs during lactation.

Many doctors and pharmacists refer to *The Physicians' Desk Reference* or similar books when seeking more information about a drug. THE BREASTFEEDING ANSWER BOOK notes that these books "which consist of information provided by drug companies, should be used with caution, as their recommendations are influenced by the companies' legal liability. In some of these sources, drug evaluations are based largely on fear of litigation rather than an objective weighing of the benefits of breastfeeding against the potential risks of the drug. The information is often overly cautious, with the underlying premise being that drugs that have not been absolutely proven safe should not be taken by a breastfeeding mother."

Sheila Stubbs of Ontario, Canada developed a serious health problem that required medication. Learning more about the drug helped her continue to nurse her daughter, even though the doctor had suggested weaning.

 Last year I noticed I was feeling tired all the time. At first I thought it was just the post-Christmas let-down, but when it continued I thought it was just plain laziness.

As the weeks passed, I began to feel a tightness in my chest and gradually it became more difficult to breathe deeply. When I got to the point that I was waking several times during the night, gasping for breath, my doctor ordered x-rays and sent me immediately to a heart specialist.

The cardiologist diagnosed pericarditis. This meant that the membrane that surrounds the heart was inflamed and there was a build-up of fluid. He prescribed a corticosteroid, prednisone, that would reduce the inflammation.

"Oh, by the way," he said, "You'll have to quit breastfeeding."

As scared as I was to find out that there was a problem with my heart, the thought of abruptly weaning my eighteen-month-old was worse. Since I had been feeling so ill, I had spent a lot of time in the past several weeks just sitting and nursing Lisa. How could I keep my little girl busy and entertained so that she wouldn't want to nurse when I was so sick myself? How could I hold her in my arms and refuse to let her nurse? How would I ever get her to sleep at bedtime, I wondered? Lisa had always nursed to sleep. What would I do with her in the middle of the night when she woke up and I couldn't nurse her quickly back to sleep?

I had nursed my other three children, so by this time I nursed without giving it a second thought. That meant I would even have to change the type of clothes I wore so I wouldn't "accidentally" nurse before I realized what I was doing. I also wondered what the hormonal changes that would follow abrupt weaning would do to my physical as well as my emotional health.

The doctor really had no idea of the effect an abrupt weaning would have on me, my daughter, and my entire family. He said she'd forget all about nursing in a few days. He said weaning wouldn't make any difference to her because, after all, we were surely "bonded" by now. He also felt that she didn't really require nursing at this point anyway, and continuing to do so would be more for my benefit than for hers.

I was sobbing when I left the doctor's office and couldn't think straight. My husband stopped at the drugstore to buy a bottle for Lisa, the first one we had ever bought. I was insulted to think that this plastic thing could be considered a substitute for our nursing relationship.

When I arrived home, I was still upset and called the Breastfeeding Clinic at the Sick Children's Hospital in Toronto for more information about prednisone and breastfeeding. They told me I could continue to nurse my baby and sent me a copy of the page from Drugs in Pregnancy and Lactation that referred to studies that have shown no harmful effects to the breastfed child if the mother is taking prednisone.

I shared this information with my cardiologist and my family doctor, but they were not at all happy with my decision to continue nursing. However, I have learned that:

> I have the right to make my own decision regarding my health care.

> Doctors are not likely to have any idea of the complex nature of the breastfeeding relationship. (Imagine telling me to wean as casually as if they were telling me to quit biting my nails!)

> A sudden, abrupt weaning can be more harmful to the child than the temporary side-effects of some drugs.

Exploring all options and getting a second or third opinion are worth the effort.

Continuing to nurse relaxed me, ensured I got plenty of rest, and kept my toddler close at hand. I experienced several side-effects from the drug, but they have all cleared up now that I am off the medication and everything is back to normal. Lisa suffered no effects from my medication.

Mother requires diagnostic tests

Most diagnostic tests and procedures will not interfere with breastfeeding. Procedures that are safe while nursing include standard x-rays, CAT scans, and ultrasounds. Barium testing, where barium is ingested to produce an image of the digestive system, does not affect breastfeeding. Magnetic resonance imaging (MRI) will not affect breastfeeding or the mother's milk, and though there are no studies at this time on the effects of the dye injected during the procedure, there are no reports of adverse reactions.

Breast tests and surgery. Tests on breast tissue such as mammograms, ultrasounds, and fine-needle aspiration of cysts do not require weaning. Mothers will want to nurse immediately before a mammogram, to reduce the amount of milk in the breast and make the procedure more comfortable. The results are best interpreted by a physician experienced in reading a mammogram of a lactating breast, since the tissue is more dense. Fine needle aspiration can be done almost painlessly in the doctor's office without a local anesthetic.

If breast surgery is needed, ask the surgeon to take care so that few milk ducts and major nerves are damaged. If the location of an incision necessitates temporary weaning, the baby can continue to nurse on the other breast. When mothers nurse on one side only, the breast that is not receiving any stimulation gradually stops making milk, while the milk supply in the other breast increases to meet the baby's demand. Many mothers and many physicians are not aware that one-sided nursing is possible. (For a story from a mother who weaned temporarily for breast surgery, see the section titled "Temporary weaning" in Chapter 5, "Gently Encouraging Weaning.")

Radioactive testing. Diagnostic tests using radioactive compounds will require you to wean temporarily. The length of time that you will not be able to nurse depends on the type of radioactive compound used. Discuss this with your doctor or radiologist ahead of time so that he or she can choose a compound that will allow you to resume breastfeeding as soon as possible. Your doctor or the radiologist supervising the treatment can advise you as to when it is safe to resume nursing. Pumping your milk and discarding it will help clear the radioactive material more quickly, as well as maintain your milk supply. You may even be able to bring milk samples to the radiology lab for testing. When radioactive compounds are used for treatment, weaning will be necessary. It may take weeks or months for the milk to be clear of radioactivity. In this situation, some mothers have elected to maintain their milk supply by pumping and discarding the milk, even for several months.

        If you or your doctor need more information about the effects of a particular test on breastfeeding, contact your local La Leche League Leader or the La Leche League International Center for Breastfeeding Information (see the resource list at the end of the chapter). THE BREAST-FEEDING ANSWER BOOK also contains information about specific tests and their effects on breastfeeding.

Mother requires hospitalization

What do you do if you must be hospitalized while your baby is nursing and not yet ready to wean? The circumstances of your hospitalization make a big difference in your choices.

        If you are hospitalized suddenly due to a medical emergency or accident, you have little or no time to make arrangements for your baby or nursing toddler. In this situation, you (or someone helping you) can ask if your child can be brought to you for nursing. You may even be able to arrange for a nursing baby to stay in your hospital room with you, although you will probably need a volunteer helper with you full-time to care for the baby. If this is not possible, you'll want to obtain an automatic breast pump. The hospital may have a pump available for your use, or your helper can rent one and bring it to the hospital. (See the resource list at the end of the chapter for more information on renting pumps.) If you are unable to pump by yourself, ask a nurse for assistance. Medical personnel may not understand or agree with you about the importance of keeping up your milk supply, but in your conversations with them you can emphasize that pumping is important to prevent engorgement, plugged ducts, and breast infections, which could slow your recovery. Check with the doctor regarding the medications you are being given to be sure they are compatible with breastfeeding.

        If you cannot arrange to see your baby for a few days, don't despair. Most babies will gladly resume nursing when you return home, although some may require gentle encouragement. Your child will miss you during the time you are in the hospital, but the loving relationship the two of you share will help to heal the hurts when you return.

        If you know ahead of time that you are going to be hospitalized for tests or surgery, you have a greater opportunity to plan and prepare for your baby's needs. In most situations, breastfeeding mothers can nurse soon after surgery, once they are alert and awake after anesthesia. If at all possible, choose outpatient surgery and arrange for help at home afterwards. Being able to rest in your own bed and nurse lying down is helpful and reassuring for both you and your baby. If you must stay overnight or longer in the hospital, it may be possible for someone to bring your baby to you, or perhaps your baby can stay in the room with you, along with someone to care for her. Some hospitals are more flexible about this than others. Call the hospital directly to find out about policies regarding breastfeeding mothers. If the hospital has a lactation consultant on staff, she may be able to help you make arrangements for breastfeeding.

Talk to your doctor about your concerns for continued nursing. Mothers have found many innovative ways to preserve their breastfeeding relationship despite the difficulties of hospitalization. For tips on being an effective advocate for yourself or family members in health care settings, read the La Leche League International pamphlet "Babies and Children in the Hospital." (See reference list at the end of the chapter for more information.)

Some mothers feel overwhelmed when faced with illness or surgery, and either don't want to continue nursing or don't feel that they can overcome the obstacles they face. Before making the decision to wean, consider what your previous weaning plans had been, and consider whether you might later regret weaning. Nursing can be easier than chasing a toddler, and weaning could be difficult when you are already feeling stressed and worried.

Weaning because of a breast infection

Some mothers wonder if they should wean when they encounter problems with plugged ducts or breast infections (also called mastitis). You'll recognize a plugged duct as a tender, reddened area in the breast. Milk is not draining properly here, and the result is soreness and inflammation. A plugged duct can turn into a breast infection, with a fever and an achy, flu-like tiredness.

This is a time when you definitely should not wean. Continuing to nurse your baby frequently on the affected breast will help relieve plugged ducts and keep the milk flowing. Abrupt weaning will make the symptoms much worse. There is no danger to the baby.

To treat a plugged duct or breast infection, apply heat to the affected area. To do this you can soak the breast in a basin of warm water or in a warm bath or shower. Or use a hot water bottle or a heating pad. Get lots of rest, but continue to nurse the baby frequently, offering the affected breast first. Gently massage the sore area before feedings and try different nursing positions to get the milk flowing. Many mothers find that if they notice the sore spot early enough, going to bed with their baby for the day, nursing frequently, and applying heat are all that's needed to clear up a

mothers have found many ways to preserve their breastfeeding relationship despite the difficulties of hospital- ization.

plugged duct or the beginnings of a breast infection. However, if you have a fever over 101°F (38.5°C) contact your doctor, who may prescribe an antibiotic. Ask for a medication compatible with breastfeeding.

Plugged ducts are often caused by an irregular nursing pattern or skipped feedings. Holidays, vacations, moving, and stress can increase the likelihood of mastitis. Other causes include a tight bra that puts pressure on the milk ducts or a baby who is not nursing effectively, perhaps because of being improperly positioned at the breast.

Frequent bouts of mastitis can be discouraging, and it may seem as if weaning is the only way to get relief. Instead of weaning, do some detective work to see if you can determine what is contributing to the reoccurrence. In many cases of recurrent mastitis, mothers find they have never gotten rid of the original infection. Taking the full course of antibiotics is necessary to cure a breast infection completely. Or the doctor may need to prescribe a different antibiotic. Many mothers find they have to change their expectations about what they can handle while their babies are young so that they can get more rest and nurse more regularly. A La Leche League Leader or lactation consultant can give you more ideas about how to prevent recurring mastitis.

Weaning if baby is ill

If your baby is ill, breastfeeding can almost always continue, and will help your baby to recover more quickly. Not only is your baby getting excellent, easy-to-digest nutrition, but your milk is also supplying your baby with antibodies and other immune factors that will help to speed the healing process. And most physicians will agree that a baby who is battling illness does not need the added stress of an abrupt weaning.

Some doctors will suggest that a child who is vomiting or has diarrhea should not receive any milk products, including human milk. However, research has shown that babies who continue to breastfeed recover more quickly from bouts of diarrhea. As a general rule, if a sick baby can take any nourishment at all by mouth, she can continue to receive human milk. If vomiting after feedings is a problem, a mother can pump or hand-express much of the milk before offering her breast. The baby can then suck for comfort while receiving only a trickle of milk.

If your baby requires surgery, you should be able to continue breastfeeding. You will want to ask your doctor how long the baby needs to fast before surgery. Recent research suggests that breastfeeding babies may need to fast for only two to three hours before anesthesia, since human milk is digested quickly. You should also be able to nurse in the recovery room as soon as your baby regains consciousness. Some babies will only hold the breast in their mouth without sucking, but they take comfort in the familiar closeness.

If your baby is hospitalized, you can make arrangements to stay overnight with your baby in the hospital. This will ease fears for both of you and allow you to continue to nurse. If your child is an older nursling, it may be more difficult for those caring for your child to take her breastfeeding needs seriously. Carefully explain your view that weaning will happen when your child is ready, and allow the medical staff to see how easily your child is comforted by nursing. Also, you may want to point out that whatever this person's views on long-term nursing, weaning right now would only add stress to an already stressful situation. Several mothers have reported that their nursing children healed so quickly and were so easy to care for in the hospital that the medical staff was amazed!

In these or any other situations where you are uncertain about your doctor's advice, it is important to communicate your concerns. Some ideas on how to do this are found at the beginning of this section. More specific information is available in THE WOMANLY ART OF BREASTFEEDING and in the La Leche League International pamphlet "Babies and Children in the Hospital." (See the reference list at the end of the chapter for more information.)

Weaning due to child's tooth decay

When a nursing toddler has evidence of tooth decay, it is not uncommon for the dentist to recommend weaning. The vast majority of breastfeeding children have no tooth decay, and rarely is breastfeeding the only culprit in dental caries. Infrequent brushing, too many sweets and juices, bacteria in the mouth, and genetic and prenatal factors all contribute to decay. You may want to speak to your dentist about options besides weaning. A trial period of a few months while you clean your child's teeth more frequently and watch her diet may prove to your dentist that weaning is not necessary to improve your child's dental health.

Renee Cox of Michigan writes about her experience with dental caries in her breastfeeding son:

"Are you willing to stop breastfeeding William?"

This question was asked in the most unlikely of places—the pediatric dentist's office! My daughter, Katherine, who is four now, had numerous cavities and even has one crown, so I was sure to bring William in for his first checkup as soon as his first teeth appeared at about one year. At that point I heard the bad news: four cavities in the top front teeth.

After identifying the cavities, Dr. Hale and I began talking. What could be the cause of dental caries at such an early age? William's having so many cavities was somewhat surprising. It was not as if I was feeding him candy, marshmallows, and ice cream for breakfast, lunch, and dinner! In fact, William had very few sweets and very little juice (he drank mostly water instead). He did nurse on demand, and William slept in our bed and nursed through the night.

Well, there, it was said. Dr. Hale had not been aware of this aspect of our "attachment parenting" lifestyle with Katherine, but by the time I took William in to see him, Dr. Hale and I had developed a close enough relationship that I was able to be honest with him about our family's lifestyle.

As I was later to learn, frequency of night nursing may contribute to dental caries, particularly if the baby is attached to the breast all night. It would be similar to snacking many times during the night, not brushing your teeth, and thereby providing an ideal environment for bad bacteria to flourish in your mouth. No, breast milk doesn't leak from the breast as it does from a bottle, but it may coat the teeth because the flow of saliva which helps to clean the teeth is lower at night. The pH of the mouth lowers and allows those acid-producing bacteria to flourish. Next thing you know, there are cavities. The percentage of nursing mothers and babies affected by this is very small, but our family ended up being one of the few.

When Dr. Hale asked, "Are you willing to stop breastfeeding William?" my answer was no. Breastfeeding provides the best nutrition, the best immunological defense, and it's part of our lifestyle. It's also one of the major ways I feel close to my baby. Dr. Hale's remark turned out to be just a question after all. Not a command, not an ultimatum, but one way in which Dr. Hale tried to determine my feelings on the issue. Once he heard my "no" we both tried to come up with a compromise—how to maintain the breastfeeding relationship and preserve the health of William's teeth.

Because he felt the frequency of nursing was a factor, Dr. Hale asked whether I could group breastfeeding sessions together. I'm sure Dr. Hale didn't realize the practical impossibility of this since he had never breastfed! With a clear understanding that William was going to continue to nurse on demand day and night, Dr. Hale suggested a routine in which we would try to keep his teeth immaculately clean, wipe them with a cloth after every breastfeeding, brush his teeth three to four times a day, and apply a small amount of topical fluoride (being sure to wipe off the excess fluoride). Upon hearing this I immediately felt relief. This was a solution that would allow us to continue breastfeeding as much as we needed to and have healthy teeth for William as well. Fear followed right behind. The proposed "program" sounded like far too much work. With two children and a busy schedule, would I be able to fit this in as well? William screamed through the once-a-day brushings I was already doing. But I was determined not to have William experience any more trauma beyond that of having these first four cavities filled. Since I, too, was very upset while those teeth were filled, I did not want to go through this again either.

So we started on this experimental program—wake up, brush his teeth, apply topical fluoride, nurse throughout the day, keep a dry cloth handy, wipe his teeth after every nursing (which he didn't like), go to sleep, nurse at night. I must confess that I did not wake up at night to wipe his teeth with a dry cloth. Other mothers who may have more stamina than I, go to it! But one of the reasons William is in bed with us is so he can nurse and I don't even have to wake up.

We continued this routine for three months, had a checkup and found no cavities. Then another three-month checkup and no cavities. Six months with no cavities! Both Dr. Hale and I were so happy it was as if we had won the lottery! Everyone in the office was happy for us, and even William managed a smile.

I am convinced that honest communication in which values were mutually respected made it possible to arrive at a solution. We were successful beyond my wildest dreams, and I can only hope our story helps other families in similar situations. While the solution or technique to resolve dental caries may not be the same in every situation, communication that respects everyone's values is an essential ingredient in the resolution process.

And yes, William still protests through every brushing, but at twenty-one months old he still nurses on demand, is cavity-free, and oh, he has the sweetest smile.

References

American Academy of Pediatrics Work Group on Breastfeeding. Breastfeeding and the use of human milk. *Pediatrics* 1997;100:1035-39.

American Academy of Pediatrics Committee on Drugs. The transfer of drugs and other chemicals into human milk. *Pediatrics* 1994; 93(1):137-50. (Reprinted in THE BREASTFEEDING ANSWER BOOK, rev. ed. by N. Mohrbacher and J. Stock. Schaumburg, IL: La Leche League International, 1997, 525-38.)

Anderson, P. Drug use during breastfeeding. *Clin Pharmacy* 1991; 10:594-623.

Briggs, B., Freeman, R., and Yaffe, S. *Drugs in Pregnancy and Lactation,* 4th ed. Baltimore/London: Williams and Wilkins, 1994.

Cox, Renee. Coping with dental caries. NEW BEGINNINGS 1997; 14(1): 10-12.

Hale, T. *Medications and Mother's Milk,* 7th ed. Amarillo, Texas: Pharmasoft, 1998-99. Also see Dr. Hale's website at http://www.ttuhsc.edu/lact/index.html

Ito, S. et al. Prospective follow-up of adverse reactions in breast-fed infants exposed to maternal medication. *Am J Obstet Gynecol* 1993; 168(5):1393-99.

Kacew, S. Adverse effects of drugs and chemicals in breast milk on the nursing infant. *J Clin Pharmacol* 1993; 33:213-21.

Lawrence, R.A. and Lawrence, R.M. *Breastfeeding: A Guide for the Medical Profession,* 5th ed. St. Louis: Mosby, 1999.

Mohrbacher, N. and Stock, J. THE BREASTFEEDING ANSWER BOOK. Schaumburg, IL: La Leche League International, 1997, 507.

Popper, Barbara. *Babies and Children in the Hospital.* Schaumburg, IL: La Leche League International, 1998.

Popper, Barbara. *The Hospitalized Nursing Baby: Meeting the Needs of Mothers, Babies, and Families in Health Care Settings.* La Leche League International Lactation Consultant Series. Schaumburg, IL: La Leche League International, 1998.

Riordan, J. and Auerbach, K. *Breastfeeding and Human Lactation,* 2nd ed. Boston and London: Jones and Bartlett, 1999.

Sears, W. NIGHTTIME PARENTING: HOW TO GET YOUR BABY AND CHILD TO SLEEP. Schaumburg, IL: La Leche League International, 1985.

US Pharmacopeial Convention. *United States Phamacoepia Dispensing Information: Drug Information for the Health Care Professional,* 16th ed. Rockville, Maryland: US Pharmacopeial Convention, 1996.

Resources

For information on breastfeeding in challenging situations contact:

Center for Breastfeeding Information, La Leche League International, P. O. Box 4079, Schaumburg, IL 60168-4079. Phone 847-519-7730. Fax 847-519-0035. Email cbi@llli.org

For information on buying or renting a breast pump contact:

Medela
P.O. Box 660
McHenry, IL 60051-0660 USA
Telephone: 1-800-435-8316

Hollister Incorporated
2000 Hollister Drive
Libertyville, IL 60048 USA
Telephone: 1-800-323-4060

chapter 9 • mothers' feelings about weaning

Weaning is an emotional topic for everyone concerned—mother, baby, father, and others close to them. Some mothers find themselves feeling very sad about the prospect of weaning, while others may look forward to calling their bodies their own once more. A desire to be finished with nursing on the mother's part is not unusual, yet many mothers are also troubled by their ambivalence about continuing to nurse. Once a mother has begun to encourage weaning, she may feel relieved, hopeful, sad, frustrated, or exhausted. Acknowledging these feelings can help you know how to handle them. This chapter looks at mothers' feelings in a variety of nursing and weaning situations. You'll also find suggestions here that will help you feel more comfortable with your decisions about nursing and weaning.

Worries about Continuing to Nurse

Mothers sometimes consider weaning because they have doubts about continuing to nurse. If you don't know anyone who is nursing a child as old as yours, it's common to wonder if you're doing the right thing. Scary little worries like "He'll never wean" or "I'm making her too dependent" or "He'll turn out odd for having nursed so long" can wake a nursing mother up in the middle of the night in a cold sweat.

Self-doubt is intensified when a mother is criticized by others, especially if the critics are vocalizing the mothers' own unspoken fears. People who may have been supportive or understanding of a nursing baby may turn critical once a child passes his first birthday. For many mothers, this is the hardest part of toddler nursing, and it's a common reason for mothers to wean a child who is past one. It's not easy to continue to nurse when people around you frown on your choice or misunderstand your motivation to continue to provide for your child's needs.

Anxieties grow when they are left unacknowledged. It may help you to write your concerns down on paper where they will likely look less intimidating. Talking with a sympathetic person who is comfortable with older children nursing can also help. Having support is the best way to deal with worries about nursing a toddler. The support of like-minded friends, books, and family is invaluable. While you may feel out of step with the mainstream, you'll know that you're not alone.

you can boost your self-confidence by seeking out support and information.

Often mothers find the support and understanding they need in a La Leche League Group where they find other mothers who are nursing toddlers. Many La Leche League Leaders have nursed older children and will listen with compassion and understanding to your fears and worries. Hearing someone else express the same feelings, struggles, and joys can help you appreciate your little nursing person all the more, and will also give you the perspective you need to decide whether or not weaning is a good solution for you and your child.

Most mothers have questions and doubts. It's a positive sign, an indication that you are a conscientious mother. But life is so much easier when doubts are put to rest and a mother can parent confidently. Confidence comes naturally with experience and the passage of time, but you can boost your self-confidence by seeking out support and information and taking care of yourself in other ways. When you are well-informed, well-rested, and have someone supportive to talk with during the day, those middle-of-the-night fears won't get out of hand.

Avoiding criticism from others

When a mother breastfeeds her baby into toddlerhood, she may find her feelings about nursing change. Certainly the feelings of people around her may change. Mothers who may have been comfortable breastfeeding almost anywhere, including public places, may now hesitate to nurse a walking, talking child around others, for fear of what they will think or say. There are probably more mothers nursing past a year than we realize, as most mothers revert to "closet nursing" after a year or two. Very few mothers ever share information about nursing past a year unless they know they are talking to the mother of another nursing toddler.

Many mothers have found ways to make nursing a toddler a more private experience. One way is to teach your child to call nursing by a special code name. It saves embarrassment for mother when her two-year-old demands "me-me" at the store, as most people never guess what he's asking for. This is especially helpful if your child likes to talk to other people. Your neighbor, who assumes you've weaned, will not catch on when your child says, "I love to have 'dis' in bed!" My first encounter with a nursing toddler and a code word was when I was pregnant with my first child. We were visiting with friends when their two-year-old asked for "honey." My husband thought that our friend carried honey in her purse—until the toddler began to nurse!

Teaching your child nursing manners is another strategy for sparing yourself embarrassment. It can be embarrassing in public settings to have your toddler pull up your blouse, put his hand inside your shirt, or in some way physically initiate nursing. To avoid this, many mothers teach their child to ask to nurse verbally. If your child wants to unbutton your blouse, you may want to consistently remind her, "Ask with words to have 'nu-nu,'" and give her something else to unbutton!

It is also a good idea to nurse at home the way you expect your child to nurse in public. Many toddlers want to push up mother's shirt, play with the other side, kneel, twist, and turn while nursing. If you value nursing discreetly in public, you will want to be consistent about nursing discreetly at home as well.

For many mothers, nursing a toddler means restricting nursing to private places. Instead of nursing wherever there's a place to sit down, mothers become more choosy about when and where to nurse. Comfort levels are vastly different—some mothers think nothing of nursing a two-year-old in most settings, others weigh each situation individually. Some mothers will nurse confidently in anonymous public situations, but would never nurse in front of a disapproving family member.

Sometimes it's too hard on the young toddler to wait to nurse in a private place. This often means that a mother ends up nursing in a place where she is not completely comfortable and is worried about reactions from others. Mothers encounter this difficulty particularly during the second twelve months of a child's life. Norma Jane Bumgarner writes about this in MOTHERING YOUR NURSING TODDLER:

The second year is the period in which you are most likely to encounter questions and criticism about your little one's continued nursing. He is, as I have said, still very much a baby and still likely to find himself needing to nurse anywhere and everywhere, without regard to how you feel about the people nearby. This is not true for all nurslings this age, but for most of them it is. Few one-year-olds have the verbal or social understanding to respond reliably to explanations and delays. With babies in the second year it is frequently easier and more peaceful, and certainly kinder to the child, just to nurse whenever and where he needs it, and deal as pleasantly as you can with any questions or criticism you receive on those occasions when privacy is just not available.

It is too bad that we must cope with something so unnatural as a widespread belief that we should not nurse our babies, and that our one-year-olds are not babies anyway. For little people in their second year of life offer their parents so much pleasure with their wide-eyed trust and exuberance. If we can rise above any criticism we may meet, we can enjoy our babies as babies far longer than many people think possible or advisable. How satisfying it is for babies—and for parents—not to have to rush through babyhood, no matter who says we should.

Think ahead about how you will answer questions or criticism. Be prepared with the words you will use. It can be helpful to answer lightly and with humor and then change the subject. You might want to deflect criticism with a comment such as "We're in the process of weaning." You can reflect you own confidence about meeting your child's needs by saying "For right now, nursing is important to him" or "Nursing makes life easier for both of us."

Sometimes a mother may go ahead and nurse her child in a setting where she is sure someone will disapprove, only to receive some unexpected support. Ruth Penick of Ohio shares this experience:

When my oldest daughter was fifteen months old I had an experience I will never forget. We were at the airport waiting for my mother's plane to arrive. Reni decided she needed to nurse, and it got to the point where I would either have to nurse her or cope with a screaming toddler. There was no good secluded place to take her and not even a place I could sit with my back to most of the activity. So we sat there in the middle of everything and nursed. After we were finished a lady in her seventies came up to me and very quietly said something to the effect that she liked to see parents putting the needs of their children ahead of what other people might think. I hope she realizes how much it meant and still means to me that she took a moment to tell me that.

It helps to remember that unlike breastfeeding a newborn, toddler nursing is no longer about nursing on demand in all situations. Mother has needs, too, and it's good to come to an agreement with your child about where and when nursing is permissible. This is easier than it sounds. When we listen to and observe our children, they give us plenty of clues to what they need and what restrictions are workable for them.

Dealing with Negative Feelings about Nursing

Sometimes mothers want to wean because they feel "tied down," they "want their bodies back," or they feel "burned-out." Sometimes a mother wants to wean because she feels overwhelmed. Too many stresses and changes in a short period of time can leave a woman looking for something—anything—in her life she can control. If she finds herself stewing about all the things she can't do because she's nursing, she may hope that weaning will allow her to put her life back together.

In all of this, a mother is longing for freedom. If this is how you feel, weaning might look like a way to gain independence from your child. But think again. Whether you are nursing or not, you are still a mother. And when children are small, they expect that their needs will most often be met by their mother. As Anne Boyd of Alabama writes, this is no easy task, but it is an important one:

 Certainly, parenting requires that a great deal of time be invested in the early years. It takes an enormous amount of energy to nurse and rock for forty-five minutes to get baby to sleep, only to have a three-year-old wake up and need mother, too. It takes great patience to demonstrate to a toddler "why we don't hit" and show alternatives.

There must be some reason why we do this. I think that many of us nurture our babies and children the way we do because we value them as human beings. We see beyond the short-term to the long-term rewards of security, independence, and self-esteem in our children.

Even mothers who place a high priority on meeting their children's emotional needs may sometimes feel desperate for freedom. If you are looking for a sense of yourself as someone other than "Mommy," you are not alone. Many mothers have these feelings and find the intensity of them comes and goes. But even if you wean, your child's needs will continue, and it will still be your job to meet them. It can be easier for you to meet your child's needs by continuing to nurse, and the ease with which nursing allows you to meet those needs can be liberating.

Many mothers look for ways to satisfy their own needs while continuing to nurse their child. Choosing to spend your child's naptime reading or doing a project, instead of doing housework, is a favorite strategy of many mothers. Some mothers, especially those with only one child, are happiest when they get out daily. Others feel better if their balance leans toward staying home. You may find a volunteer opportunity you can fit in around your child's needs, or one where you can take your child with you.

Being aware of and honest about your own needs is the best way to avoid feeling burned-out or put upon by a nursing toddler. Taking care of yourself may be easier now than when your child was a baby, as he may enjoy dad's company more, allowing you to spent short periods of time away from him. Mary Fleming of Illinois writes about how she worked through "nursing burn-out":

 I have experienced different stages of nursing burn-out with each of my nursing experiences. I have found that my desire to wean my children has always coincided with the times when I am neglecting my own needs. With small children in the house, mother's needs often come last. I used to feel selfish when I took time for myself. I have finally realized that when I nurture myself, I have so much more to give to other members of my family. There are many ways I have found to nurture myself, without shorting anyone in my family:

> *Long aromatherapy baths right after my husband comes home from work*
>
> *Taking a yoga class once a week*
>
> *Reading science fiction novels in the middle of the night*
>
> *Hiring a babysitter to take the children to the park one afternoon a week*
>
> *Riding my bicycle for a half-hour*
>
> *Getting a massage as a special treat*
>
> *Arranging with my husband for a sleep-in morning on the weekend*
>
> *Napping when the baby naps.*

You can get some perspective on nursing burn-out by realizing that the years in which you have a nursing baby or child are a very small part of your life. If you live to be seventy-five and nurse two children three years apiece, you will still spend sixty-nine years of your life not nursing!

Feeling manipulated

At times, some mothers will feel resentment about continuing to nurse. They may feel they're being controlled or manipulated by their child, particularly if the child nurses frequently or often asks to nurse when the mother is busy with other activities or is somewhere out in public. Some children have irritating or exacting nursing habits, such as wanting to play with the other nipple or wanting to nurse only in a certain chair. This can leave a mother feeling as if she is at her child's mercy. Yet mothers in these situations may also feel guilty about wanting to wean, especially if their child isn't ready or a mother had thought previously she would practice natural weaning.

If your child is very attached to nursing, yet you are longing to wean, it can feel as though there's no way to resolve the problem except to force the issue. In this kind of confrontation, it seems that one of you must win and one of you will have to lose. Looking instead for a "win-win" solution may help you feel more at peace.

Extended nursing isn't about being a martyr or feeling powerless in your nursing relationship. Children pick up on these feelings readily, and either distance themselves or cling more desperately. If you're feeling resentful, it might be helpful to first try seeing your child in a different light. Instead of seeing nursing (or not nursing) as a power struggle to be won or lost, consider that your child is asking to nurse in order to get his needs met. Are you often busy or distracted? Is nursing the only way he can get your attention? If you offered to join him on the floor and build with blocks or read a story to him instead, would he be just as happy? Or perhaps your child's intense feelings about nursing are part of his personality. High-need or "spirited" children often need more of everything—more comfort, more reassurance, more sucking, just plain more nursing.

You may also find it helpful to set some limits on nursing for your child, particularly in relation to what you find difficult in your nursing relationship. Some limits mothers have found helpful are: nursing only at home, nursing only at certain times of the day, and no fiddling with mother's body while nursing. (Help your child find something besides you to fiddle with while he nurses.)

> extended nursing isn't about being a martyr or feeling powerless in your nursing relationship.

Frustrations over fertility

Some mothers start to think seriously about weaning when they want to conceive their next child. For most mothers, fertility naturally returns after their baby starts solids or other supplements, begins to sleep through the night, or nurses less as he gets older. When exactly a mother becomes fertile again is highly individual, and breastfeeding mothers report that they begin to menstruate again anywhere from three months to two years after their child is born. A few mothers do not have periods until their child weans entirely. Some women may have regular menstrual periods while nursing and still experience difficulty getting pregnant.

If your biological clock is ticking, it can seem impossible or impractical to wait until your child weans naturally to become pregnant again. Mothers have employed a variety of personal answers and strategies in this area. Some find cutting back on the frequency of nursing (once their child is eating other foods well) causes their fertility to return. Weaning from night nursing is another possible strategy to encourage the return of fertility. Some mothers choose to keep nursing and find they eventually get pregnant without having to wean. Other mothers wean, get pregnant, and are happy with their decision. A few wean and find it still takes a long time to get pregnant or don't conceive at all, and end up regretting weaning. Some mothers must wean entirely to become fertile again, even if they're ovulating.

In some cases, mothers choose to approach the situation more spiritually. They believe if they haven't become fertile again, there is a reason. Others look to the child they have now, see the child's need to nurse, and let go of their own desire to control when they will conceive again.

Making a decision in this area is stepping into the unknown, as much of mothering is. Trusting your heart and looking to the needs of your family will help you to find an answer that feels right.

Weaning to Improve a Child's Behavior

Sometimes weaning seems to be the only answer to challenging behaviors in a nursing child. Mothers hope that weaning will put an end to certain problems they may be having with their child, such as when a child wakes frequently at night, or bites the breast during feedings. It is tempting to blame childish behavior on nursing, but looking at the whole picture, instead of just at nursing, may give you a clearer understanding of your child and of yourself.

Weaning and night-waking

If your child is waking often at night to nurse, you are probably wondering if weaning would help him sleep better. Night-waking is a common occurrence in many babies and children and may continue for months and even years. Dr. William Sears explains that babies aren't designed to sleep through the night, but to sleep in short periods broken by frequent nursing. It would be easier for us as parents if our babies slept more like we do, but it's not in the best interest of babies. Frequent nursing contributes to better growth in the early months. Sleeping less soundly may even offer protection against Sudden Infant Death Syndrome (SIDS). Needs are no less intense for children during the night than they are during the day. Once they are older and busy during the day, they may be waking frequently because they are receiving the majority of their mother's milk at night. Older children often wake for other reasons as well: teething, colds, minor tummy aches, allergies, and loneliness are possibilities.

Many people think babies and toddlers wake up only to nurse, and would not wake anymore if they were weaned. For some children, weaning does lessen night-waking. But for others, weaning doesn't necessarily bring sleep. Your weaned child may still wake at night, and the night-waking will be more difficult for you because you no longer have a guaranteed way to put him back to sleep. While there may be some ways you can help your child to sleep better now, keep in mind that all children will indeed sleep through the night eventually. In my family, my sons "weaned" from night-waking in the same way and in the same time frame as they weaned from the breast. Gradually, over a few years, they grew into sleeping through the night. They acquired the skill naturally, at their own pace, and have been sound sleepers ever since.

If you are tired from getting up with your baby at night, look for ways to help yourself feel more rested. You might try taking your child into your bed, or having him sleep on a mattress on the floor next to your bed so you can nurse lying down and fall back to sleep. During the day, take advantage of your baby's naptimes to rest. Avoiding caffeine and getting some exercise during the day can help you sleep better at night and fall back to sleep more easily when your baby wakes. Don't check the clock when you wake at night, don't count how many times you are awakened, and don't dwell on how much sleep you didn't get. Keeping a mental tally will only make you feel more tired.

Sometimes you can adjust your child's daytime activities to encourage better sleeping at night. Some children are overstimulated by too many daytime activities and sleep better after a quiet day at home. Other mothers find that spending time outside every day improves their child's sleep. Maybe your child needs to eat more during the day, or drink more water. Susan Van Meter from Massachusetts was struggling with night-waking, and found that her daytime routine was a contributing factor.

 Even though Rebecca had not been indicating a need to nurse more frequently during the day, I instinctively felt that too little time with mother was the culprit for restless nights. I immediately stopped worrying about what needed to be done around the house and parked myself in the nursing rocker and let her nurse for an extended time at naptimes and bedtime. After the first day there was an immediate improvement in her sleep cycles! The additional milk, sucking, and time in mother's arms seem to have done the trick.

Some mothers choose to wean from nighttime nursings, but not to wean altogether. This works with some children, but may be very difficult with others. Mothers who try this talk about their plans with their child during the day. They may ask dad to help them comfort the child during the night, and they are prepared to lose some sleep for a few nights in order to help their child adjust to the change. Lynn Mazza of Vermont writes about helping her two-year-old son sleep through the night.

 When my son was 27 months old, he was waking every half hour to two hours at night. Feeling sleep-deprived, frustrated, and resentful, I decided to wean from night nursing. It helped me to be clear about my reasons. A sleepy, grumpy, resentful mom is not the kind of mother I wanted to be. Knowing this gave me the resolve I needed.

I began to prepare my son. I told him that in three more nights I wasn't going to give him "num-nums" if he woke up when it was still dark. I thought it was important to give him a concrete time frame. I explained that "num-nums" needed to rest to make enough milk. For three nights, I repeated this information until the big night when I told him the time had come. I presented him with his very own Mickey Mouse water bottle to keep next to our bed in case he was thirsty when he woke in the middle of the night. I told him he could nurse again when it was light outside. Since it was summer and nights were shorter, this allowed him to nurse very early in the morning. A different concrete reference point, such as when Dad gets up for work or when the dog barks at the newspaper carrier, could work for another child.

The first night was very difficult. My husband stayed beside us in our family bed, and I held our little one, rocked him, sympathized with him, and loved him. But I didn't nurse him. By the third night he had the idea. He still woke up once or twice at night, but without tears. He did learn to go back to sleep without nursing. He was never left to cry alone, and the concrete time frames and extra love he received at night and during the day helped him take this big step. Since he made the adjustment in just a few days, I feel that he was developmentally and emotionally ready.

Chapter 5, "Gently Encouraging Weaning," has other suggestions that may be helpful. In nighttime weaning, as with other phases of weaning, remember to be flexible. If not being able to nurse at night causes your child great distress, or if he becomes more clingy during the day, you will want to reconsider your decision about nighttime nursing.

For more information on night-waking, see NIGHTTIME PARENTING by William Sears, MD, and *Crying Baby, Sleepless Nights* by Sandy Jones.

Weaning for relief from non-stop nursing

Babies need to breastfeed frequently in the early months in order to grow and thrive, but by the time a child is a year old, most mothers expect to nurse less frequently. Yet some toddlers seem to nurse as much as newborns. Sheila Kippley observes in *Breastfeeding and Natural Child Spacing* that "frequent nursing may continue well into the second or third year of life." She also cites a study by James Wood, a research scientist at the University of Michigan Population Studies Center. He studied the Gainj people of New Guinea who nurse their children for about three years. He noted that infants nursed about every twenty-four minutes, and three-year-olds nursed about every eighty minutes. This may give you a new perspective on how frequent is frequent.

It is wise, however, to think about why your child is nursing so often. Sometimes a child nurses frequently because it is the only meaningful contact he has with his mother. If you suspect this may be the case in your child's life, take time to play with him and to read stories together. Let him help you with housework and cooking, and make eye contact when you talk to him. If your child begins to nurse less often, you'll know you want to make an effort to continue these other activities on a regular basis.

Some toddlers nurse often due to boredom. Besides spending more time doing stimulating and interesting things together at home, you might want to go out more. Play outdoors or go to the park, visit the library and other interesting places in your town, or take your child with you on errands (or send him with dad). New sights and sounds can help relieve boredom. Often toddlers don't think to nurse when they're busy.

If your child is still determined to nurse many times a day, despite attention from you and a stimulating environment, he may well have a genuine need to nurse frequently. Intense, high-need children may need nursing to calm down and touch base with mother before they go on to enjoy other activities. Your child may have a great desire to be touched and to connect with you on a regular basis, especially if he is an extrovert who thrives on contact with other people and renews his own energy by interacting with others. Children who are very sensitive or emotional may nurse frequently to keep themselves on an even keel, or as a retreat from the stress they feel so acutely.

There may be times when a child's nursing frequency increases. If this is the case, consider these questions: Is this an emotionally stressful time for you or your child? If so, he may be nursing more often for comfort and reassurance. Is your child growing quickly, or making huge developmental strides? My children seemed to nurse more right before they mastered walking, potty-training, and other big steps in growing up. Is your child ill, teething, or coming down with a cold? Children nurse more when they don't feel well. Often, if you let a few days go by, the reason for a sudden increase in nursing frequency becomes apparent.

Weaning to improve a child's appetite

Toddlers are notorious for being picky, light eaters, whether or not they are nursing. Many mothers who nurse their toddlers are glad to be providing the superior nutrition of human milk to fill in the gaps in their child's diet. But breastfeeding alone is not sufficient nourishment for a child one year or older, and babies need to be introduced to a growing variety of other foods, beginning in the middle of the first year. However, you can be assured that when your child does nurse, the nutritional quality of your milk is excellent.

If your doctor or another advisor is urging you to wean, believing that nursing is keeping your child from having a better appetite for other foods, suggest he look at the whole child, not just his eating habits. Is your child healthy, active, and developmentally on target? Even if he is smaller or larger than what is typical for his age, these other signs are assurance that he's growing well. Continuing to nurse while your child learns to enjoy a greater variety of foods assures that he will continue to be well nourished and receive adequate calories. There are no guarantees that weaning will make his eating habits any better.

You might find your child eats better if you are flexible and offer choices. Making a wide variety of foods available, encouraging snacking, and being creative about where your child eats might help. Using different dishes, even toy dishes, cutting food in different shapes, eating outside, allowing the child to carry food around, feeding your child when he is hungry and not making him wait for a meal to be prepared are other ways to get more food into a picky toddler. For everyone's sake, try to maintain a relaxed attitude about food and not get into power struggles.

Weaning to promote independence

Some mothers feel that weaning will encourage a shy, clingy child to become more independent. If your child is more shy than most, or doesn't feel comfortable being separated from you even for short periods of time, you may think that continuing to nurse is the cause. In some respects, this may be true. Your child sees you as the secure figure in his life and the place he goes to get his most basic needs met. Therefore he wants to be near you. But this isn't a bad thing. This type of closeness between mother and child is a sign of healthy human development, and your child will feel more secure in later life if he is allowed to separate from you based on his own inner timetable.

In other respects, nursing may have little to do with a toddler or preschooler's bashful tendencies. Any mother with more than one child notices distinct personality differences between her children. Your child may be shy and sensitive by nature. Heredity may be a clue. My nursing two-year-old daughter has a shy, stay-close-to-mama manner about her. My mother says I did, too, at that age, although she was only able to nurse me for six weeks.

Weaning is unlikely to change your child's personality. In the absence of the comfort and security of nursing, you may find your child becoming even more clingy. Continuing to nurse until your child is ready to wean is the best way to give your child the security he needs to become independent.

Weaning because nursing is a "habit"

Some mothers wonder if their child has just gotten into the habit of nursing, and might be just fine if he were weaned. Occasionally, this could be the case. James L. Hymes, Jr., offers this now-classic definition of how to determine the difference between needs and habits:

> *If it was easy to break, it was a habit. If you run into any major difficulty at all, beware, you probably are not dealing with an old worn-out habit. Chances are that you are tampering with a need. Habits fade away with a little counterpush. If you ignore basic needs, or try to block them, they shoot sky high. If you treat needs as if they were habits, all you do is to make them go on longer and stronger and more powerfully than ever.*

One way to decide if your child is nursing out of habit or need is to try some gentle weaning techniques and carefully observe your child's reaction. If your child balks or becomes distressed, this may indicate that nursing is still a strong need. On the other hand, you may discover that your child is ready to wean and just needed a little assistance from you. In either case, watching your child and following his lead will save you from having to guess and worry in this situation.

When a baby bites

When a baby bites while breastfeeding, it is surprising and painful for a mother. Fortunately, babies seldom bite more than a few times. Weaning is rarely necessary, though it may take some patience and a couple of weeks to get beyond your baby's biting stage. Babies may experiment with biting when they are getting teeth, but they soon learn that mother disapproves of this behavior. The presence of teeth will not affect a baby's ability to breastfeed.

Usually, the first bite surprises the baby as much as it does you. If you reacted with surprise, your baby may have been frightened. This may be enough to prevent biting in the future. Some babies, however, delight in mother's startled reaction and try it again. If biting becomes more frequent, see if you can figure out when your baby is most likely to bite. Many bite toward the end of the feeding, or when they want to change sides, or when they're nursing only because you offered, not because they really need to at the moment. Some bite as a way of communicating their need for your attention when you are distracted by the phone or other activities while you're nursing. If your baby is a persistent biter, keep your finger on your breast near the corner of your baby's mouth, so that you can quickly break the suction and remove your breast before he clamps down. If the baby does bite, use your finger to protect your nipple as you withdraw it from his mouth. End the feeding and offer a teething toy instead. Some mothers may sit the baby on the floor briefly to give him the message that biting is not acceptable. Mothers have found that some babies bite due to a decreased milk supply, perhaps from infrequent nursing or an undetected pregnancy. Nursing whenever possible in a quiet place, without your attention distracted by television, reading, the phone, or other people, can help you focus on your baby and prevent biting from occurring.

Mothers' Feelings about Nursing and Weaning during Pregnancy

Many mothers worry that they must wean when they become pregnant or risk hurting their unborn child. In fact, most mothers have no physical problems with breastfeeding through a pregnancy and deliver healthy, normal-weight babies. Nursing mothers may find they need to consume extra calories to gain sufficient weight during pregnancy, and may choose to take vitamin supplements. Some mothers notice uterine contractions after nursing in the later part of pregnancy and may worry about premature labor. These contractions are a common occurrence during pregnancy, even if you aren't nursing, and don't cause premature labor in a normal pregnancy. Pregnancy in itself often causes women to feel fatigued, but there's no evidence that continuing to breastfeed makes this any worse. Nursing may actually make it possible to rest more with your toddler.

Some pregnant mothers are quite relieved when they are assured that they don't have to wean a child who isn't ready yet. Still they may find that nursing through a pregnancy brings some challenges, particularly nipple tenderness. Some mothers find that nipple tenderness is most intense at the beginning of a nursing session and seems to let up once they've been nursing awhile. Tenderness may decrease after the first trimester as well. Relaxation techniques may make nipple soreness easier to cope with. You may also ask your child to nurse more gently, less frequently, or for a shorter time. Further along in pregnancy, finding a new way to position the child around your expanding belly is often a challenge. Lying down to nurse might be easier and can give you an opportunity to rest.

While some mothers continue nursing because they find it easier than weaning, other mothers find breastfeeding while pregnant a difficult and even unpleasant experience. Besides experiencing sore and sensitive nipples, they may feel irritated and edgy when their child nurses. Many mothers cope with nursing during pregnancy by employing partial weaning techniques, encouraging the child to reduce the amount of time spent nursing without withdrawing breastfeeding altogether. For other mothers, a new pregnancy becomes the time to wean.

In a study of 503 La Leche League members who became pregnant while nursing, researchers found that sixty-nine percent of their babies weaned at some time during the pregnancy. This doesn't mean you can count on your child weaning naturally during pregnancy. Children wean during pregnancy for many reasons: because the mother encourages weaning, because of second-trimester changes in the quantity and taste of mother's milk, or because the child was ready to wean anyway. If you feel you want to wean because you are pregnant, employing some of the strategies in Chapter 5, "Gently Encouraging Weaning," will help you and your child to bring your breastfeeding relationship to a peaceful end.

Even if you want to continue nursing through your pregnancy, you may find your feelings change as the months progress. This is not unusual, and you may decide that you want to encourage weaning after all. If you do decide to wean, you can still meet your child's needs for love and closeness with you in other ways.

some pregnant mothers are quite relieved to know they don't have to wean a child who isn't ready yet.

Tandem nursing

Continuing to nurse through pregnancy means you may very well be nursing two when your new baby is born. This is called tandem nursing. Many mothers report that letting the older child continue to nurse helps decrease sibling rivalry by making it easier for the older child to accept the new baby. They describe how the siblings nurse together, holding hands or patting each other.

Feelings mothers associate with tandem nursing range from confidence, peace, and pleasure, to restlessness and resentment. The same mother may feel all of these emotions in the same day or week. THE BREASTFEEDING ANSWER BOOK tells about these feelings:

Many mothers are motivated to tandem nurse because they feel strongly about continuing to satisfy their older child's needs through breastfeeding. Their primary focus is on the child they know rather than on the unborn baby, who is still a stranger.

However, once a baby is born, many mothers find their feelings shift dramatically. Nature programs mothers—especially if mother and newborn get off to a good start in the early days and weeks—to become infatuated with the little one in their arms. The older child suddenly looks so big, and many mothers find that they resent taking time away from their newborn to nurse their older child.

Not every mother experiences such a dramatic shift in feelings. But when she does, she may feel guilty and alarmed—especially if she decided to tandem nurse for the sake of the older child and then feels waves of resentment at his wanting to nurse.

These opposing feelings—first protective of the older child, then resentful of his demands—are completely normal when a new baby joins the family. Even if the older child were not nursing, a mother might very well experience this kind of conflict. When the child is nursing, however, it is common for negative feelings to focus on breastfeeding. This does not mean that the mother will never enjoy nursing her older child again, but it takes a while for everyone to adjust to the new family situation.

If you feel ambivalent or mostly negative about continuing to nurse an older child after the birth of a new baby, it may be helpful to try to improve the tandem nursing situation before attempting to wean completely. The first adjustment that many mothers make is to recognize that they can't handle much more than nursing in the first few months, and when they surrender to this idea, they are much happier.

Often an older child begins to nurse more frequently after the baby is born, perhaps due to his own anxiety about his changing place in the family. Usually this increased demand for nursing is only temporary, and within a few weeks of the birth the child gradually returns to his earlier nursing pattern. Suggesting the older child limit nursing to a couple of favorite times each day may help a mother feel less overwhelmed. Decide whether you prefer nursing the two children at the same time or separately; if you don't want to nurse them together, explain to the older child that he must wait, and then be sure that he, too, gets his special time at the breast. If the older child finds waiting or other limits on nursing to be too distressing, you might decide that fewer rules are less stressful for everyone. Getting dad and older siblings to pay special attention to the older child might be helpful as well.

Franci Sassin of California writes about how she handled the challenges of nursing during a pregnancy and then nursing two:

When I was pregnant with my second child, nursing my two-and-a-half-year-old became physically uncomfortable, although before my pregnancy I had not been able to imagine not wanting to nurse him or not enjoying that part of our relationship. Fortunately, by the time the new baby was born, my older child had been asking to nurse only once a week or so. I had thought that once my milk came in and I was more comfortable physically that I wouldn't mind tandem nursing. I wasn't prepared for the strong emotions I experienced after the baby was born. I simply did not want my three-year-old nursing, but he started asking to nurse several times a day. I was getting upset and short-tempered with him, and he responded with anger to any attempt on my part to delay or refuse his requests.

I really did not want to end our nursing relationship on such a negative note. The first step to improving our situation was a compromise about when he could nurse. We agreed he would nurse in the morning when he woke up. Arriving at this compromise required lots of discussion at times when we were both rational.

My attitude improved immensely when I got my son to accept nursing to the count of ten on each side. This also seemed to decrease the physically irritating sensations I was experiencing when he nursed. Over the following months, my son gradually cut back on his requests without further pressure from me. By age four, he was back to nursing very infrequently. On his four-and-a-half birthday, we had a weaning party to officially mark the end of that chapter of our lives.

Mothers who are tandem nursing need opportunities to take care of themselves, even if only for a brief period of time. A bath alone, a short walk, time to read or chat with a friend can help you feel less overwhelmed. Eating well and drinking enough fluids are also important. Expect that it will take a month or more for all of you to adjust to the new baby and to find a workable pattern of tandem nursing. Lisa Schaeffer of Pennsylvania shares how she learned to cope with tandem nursing:

Attitude is key. Accepting and anticipating that he would ask to nurse helped me not to get so angry when he did ask. I've learned to tell my son that he cannot nurse at certain times, but then I give him a time when he can. I avoid sitting in the recliner (a popular nursing spot) if I don't want to nurse two. Other times, I sit in the recliner, prop the baby with a pillow on one side and Matthew gets his own pillow. Then I grab a book or the cordless phone and enjoy some peace and quiet. When it gets to be more than I can bear, I remind myself, "This too shall pass." Babies don't keep.

Some mothers find tandem nursing overwhelming and have strong negative feelings, even after trying to make improvements and adjustments in the situation. In those cases, gentle and gradual weaning techniques may help. Weaning an older child while you are still nursing a baby is possible, though it may require extra creativity and energy on your part.

I'm Ready to Wean, But My Child Is Not

What if, after trying many gentle weaning techniques, you still really want to wean, but it's clear that your child doesn't? This is a difficult situation to be in, but many mothers have been in your place. Balancing your needs with your child's is not impossible, but may take some time and creativity. Norma Jane Bumgarner in MOTHERING YOUR NURSING TODDLER suggests that you must decide either to be happy with weaning or happy with nursing.

Leaving the land of ambivalence makes a big difference for many mothers. Most likely, you aren't even aware of the degree of your ambivalence about nursing until it is resolved. If you are feeling defensive, inflexible, powerless, or guilty about weaning, it is likely that you are also ambivalent. Once you believe in your heart that weaning will be a positive step for you and your child, weaning will most likely proceed smoothly. How do you get to the point where the decision feels right? Over a period of time, when you are struggling, learning, and looking for answers, things slowly become clearer. You may notice the positive aspects of continuing to nurse and decide not to wean. Or you may see how weaning can happen gently and gradually and decide that this is the best answer for you, your child, and your situation. In either case, you feel at peace.

References

Berke, G. *Nursing Two, Is It for You?* (pamphlet). Schaumburg, IL: La Leche League International. 1989.

Bumgarner, N. J. MOTHERING YOUR NURSING TODDLER. Schaumburg, IL: La Leche League International, 1982, 134-35, 187-88.

Hymes, James L., Jr. *The Child Under Six,* 2nd ed. Consortium, 1994.

Kippley, S. *Breastfeeding and Natural Child Spacing: How "Ecological" Breastfeeding Spaces Babies.* Cincinnati: Couple to Couple League International, 1989, 73, 41-42.

La Leche League International. THE WOMANLY ART OF BREASTFEEDING, 6th rev. ed. Schaumburg, IL: La Leche League International, 1997, 253.

Mohrbacher, N. and Stock, J. THE BREASTFEEDING ANSWER BOOK, rev. ed. Schaumburg, IL: La Leche League International, 1997, 351.

Newton, N. and Theotokatos, M. Breastfeeding during pregnancy in 503 women: Does a psychobiological weaning mechanism exist in humans? *Emotion and Reproduction* 1979; 20B:845-49.

Sears, W. and Sears, M. *Parenting the Fussy Baby and High-Need Child.* Boston: Little-Brown, 1996.

Sears, W. NIGHTTIME PARENTING: HOW TO GET YOUR BABY AND CHILD TO SLEEP. Schaumburg, IL: La Leche League International, 1985, 17-21.

chapter 10 • when weaning isn't going well

Janet hadn't expected weaning to be so difficult. Her sixteen-month-old, Paul, wouldn't let her out of his sight. He was no longer content to stay at home with Dad when Janet went to her Thursday night class. She was spending all day on her feet, because whenever she sat down, Paul crawled into her lap to nurse. Now they both had colds, and a heavy snowstorm was expected that night. Janet was feeling trapped, overwhelmed, and uncertain what to do.

Janet and Paul are experiencing some of the warning signs that weaning isn't going well. These signs may show up in the child, the mother, and sometimes even in the rest of the family. Sometimes it is a feeling of unrest or chaos at home. Sometimes a child signals her distress by regressing in certain areas (such as toilet training) or by increased night-waking. The child may also behave uncharacteristically, such as being more fussy, cranky, or afraid of separations from mother. Other signs that weaning is distressing for the child include biting, adopting a security object, stomach aches, stuttering, constipation, or increased sucking on other things (fingers, toys, pacifier).

It may be difficult to tell if your child's behavior changes are due to weaning or should be attributed to something else. Illness and stress can also cause a child to show some of the above characteristics. If your family life is reasonably calm, and after a couple of days your child doesn't seem to be improving, you will want to consider if weaning has become an overwhelming experience for your child. Some children adapt to a mother encouraging weaning after only a few difficult days, while others are unhappy much longer.

Rose Putnam of Alaska had to wean her daughter Allison temporarily because Rose needed to take a medication. Allison would not be able to resume nursing for about two months. She relates the difficulty Allison had with weaning, and the effects of weaning on her daughter:

At fifteen months, Allison was still an avid nurser. She turned away from most other forms of nourishment and had no real desire to try most foods we had offered her up until this time. We hoped she would eat more solid food when I could not nurse her. She didn't. Most days we could get her to eat a substantial breakfast, a little lunch, but rarely any dinner.

After we stopped nursing, my smiling, sweet, happy daughter became sullen, clingy, and inconsolable. She had awful temper tantrums and a constant diaper rash. Her beautiful blue eyes became dull with black circles under them. She was listless and didn't have the spunk normally seen in toddlers her age. We did everything imaginable to try and help her through this ordeal. We took walks, played soothing music, sang, played games, and took drives in the car so she could go to sleep and get some rest. The only things that helped us cope with this were the support we got from our La Leche League Leaders and the thought that one day we would be able to resume breastfeeding and reverse these changes that had occurred in Allison. We very much wanted that "other" little girl back.

Rose was able to resume nursing Allison after seven weeks. She encouraged her to nurse at first when she was asleep.

Within a week, Allison was back to her old cheerful self. The diaper rash went away, and although she still clings to me a lot, I don't mind. Now she clings with a smile on her face and her beautiful blue eyes are bright and clear once again.

Causes of Weaning Distress

Weaning is going too quickly

Sometimes a child is upset by the pace of weaning. Even if your child seems ready to wean, it is important to give her time to get used to the changes. A child who is being weaned too quickly may show some of the signs mentioned above. If you suspect that weaning is happening too quickly, the obvious answer to the difficulties is to let your child nurse more often. Don't expect your child to give up so much of her reliance on nursing just yet. Your child may need more time to become comfortable with suitable substitutes for nursing, such as alternate ways to go to sleep or other ways to be reassured of your love and attention.

Child is feeling insecure and anxious

Insisting on nursing more and being clingy, angry, or demanding of your attention are often the child's way of asking, "Do you still love me even if you won't let me nurse? Can I still feel secure in your love?" To help your child feel loved and secure during the weaning process you'll need to focus on giving your child your attention and time in other ways. Think of simple ways to reassure your child of your love, like looking at her and really listening when she talks to you, playing with her and touching her often. Cris King of Ohio tells about her son's reaction when she encouraged him to wean:

When I tried to wean my second child at two, he wasn't ready, and his actions surprised me. He was truly mad at me. He couldn't look at me. This was an emotion we had never experienced. I talked to two La Leche League members. They could tell I was not comfortable with my decision and encouraged me to disregard the pressures of the people around me. They reminded me this was something between me and my child only. I resumed nursing and I'm glad I did.

When my son was two-and-a-half, it was the holiday season. I was so busy with work and holiday preparations, and he was distracted by all the excitement. When the holidays were over, we realized that weaning had taken place.

Too many changes at once

Have you been trying to wean in the midst of other changes in your life or your child's? Have you been trying many different weaning techniques at the same time? Too many things may be changing too quickly for your child. Take some time to evaluate your life at the moment. Is your child's life consistent and predictable from day to day? Or is your child being asked to nurse less during the day, to learn to use the toilet, and to adjust to a new puppy in the family all at once? Sometimes mothers, desperate to complete weaning, don't realize that even small changes quickly add up to a lot of stress for a child. Letting our children adjust to change slowly, one step at a time, is far more likely to bring success, and will leave everyone feeling happier. N. Zoe Hilton of Ontario, Canada, encouraged her son to wean after she became pregnant, but she found he had difficulty accepting weaning:

nursing more and being clingy are the child's way of asking, "do you still love me?"

My nipples were so sore that I couldn't bear the thought of breastfeeding. But I didn't know how I could avoid it altogether without disrupting my relationship with Nathaniel (and my sleep!) too much. So I looked for ways of limiting Nathaniel's nursing. I ended his habit of alternating breasts several times at each nursing, and I insisted that he "finish one side" then change to the other if he wanted more. This restriction caused an increase in his attempts to possess both breasts at once by playing with the unoccupied one. His poking at my nipple already bothered me, and now that I was pregnant even light touches on my breast felt like an imposition. So I also blocked his wandering hands, despite his bewilderment and angry protests. At night, I no longer picked him up when he woke up whimpering; if he wanted to nurse, he had to get up and come to me. One night, he begged to me from the other side of the family bed, "Mummy, I need to nuzzle, could you pull me over?" His sad little voice melted what little resolve I had. I had to appreciate how stressful this time was for Nathaniel, and I doubted whether I was doing the right thing.

All this change was going on at the same time as the hustle and bustle of the holidays. We like to keep all the social trimmings of the holidays fairly low key, but there were still extra trips to church and the occasional night out for adult celebrations, leaving Nathaniel screaming in the arms of a teen-aged babysitter. His demands to nurse increased.

In my desperation, I resorted to all sorts of mother substitutes. I tried soothers [pacifiers]. I tried bottles. But Nathaniel would drink a bottle of juice, a bottle of water, a bottle of milk, and at 11 PM he would still need to nurse in order to end his misery and get to sleep. I also tried rocking, walking, and singing. Since nighttime nursing was the most stressful for me, I started to eliminate night nursing and continued to nurse on demand during the day. To help clarify this new rule, I told Nathaniel that we would only nurse in the rocking chair. To him, this rule was a complete surprise and made no sense at all. He cried with heartbreaking sobs when I refused to nurse him in bed. It didn't take him long to figure out that he could circumvent the rule by asking to nurse in the rocking chair at 2 AM. I brought the rocking chair into the bedroom, rocked for an hour or two while he slept at the breast, then got back into bed. He stirred when I moved him, and finished nursing to a deeper sleep in bed. So he'd had to beg to nurse, I had lost two hours of sleep, and we ended up nursing in bed despite the rocking chair rule.

After nights of struggle, I could see that the "no nighttime nursing" rule was unworkable. If I hadn't been convinced after the rocking chair episode, I certainly was the next morning, as I lay awake hoping to drift off for another few minutes. Nathaniel got out of bed and started playing with my recorder, a wind instrument which I had owned since childhood and which Nathaniel had learned to handle with care. But that morning, I heard several loud bangs, as he threw the recorder repeatedly onto the hard floor, breaking it in two. When I asked him why he had thrown it, he replied, "Because I need to nurse."

Eventually, Zoe says, it was Nathaniel himself who convinced her that letting him wean in his own good time was the right thing to do, and together they discovered an acceptable substitute for nursing.

One night when Nathaniel awoke in the wee hours and asked to nurse, I sighed, "Oh, come on, Nathaniel, you're a big boy." The weak but honest reply came back, "Actually, I'm a little boy." It was 5:30 AM. I pulled him close to me, the tears of rejection still damp on his cheeks. He slept at my breast until dawn, and through many nights after that, until he simply stopped nursing.

Child isn't ready to wean yet

A child not able to accept substitutes for nursing is telling you she isn't ready to wean. This is the child who rarely accepts an offer to play or eat or do anything else when she wants to nurse. This may also be the child who agrees not to nurse much during the day, but then nurses all night. Seeming distressed and listless is often another sign of not being ready. Carrie Sommer of California writes about her son not being ready to wean, and the compromises she made:

By fifteen months, Drew still nursed steadily. I began to tire of being constantly in demand and of not being able to be gone for long periods of time. I resented the fact that I was the only one who could get him to sleep. One day, after an illness that had him nursing day and night, I said, "Enough is enough." I would nurse him only at night and not during the day.

Then a funny thing happened. Drew started eating better. "Oh happy day," I thought, "I'm free." But the feeling was short-lived. Drew started nursing in the evening after his bath for an hour at a time and waking every two hours during the night to nurse. Also, since he still needed naps but had to nurse to fall asleep, I found myself in the car in the middle of the day, driving around to get him to sleep.

After a month I decided this was the wrong way to go about weaning. My husband suggested resuming nursing so our household could go back to the way it used to be: partial chaos as opposed to complete chaos. I relented and began nursing during the day for naps only. This worked for a couple of weeks until one day Drew requested to nurse off my predetermined schedule. Now we were almost back to where we had started, except for two important things: first, he was still eating well and second, he was comfortable with longer periods away from me.

A friend suggested letting Drew know he could nurse for only a short amount of time and to count to a certain number before ending the sessions. It took a couple of times, and sometimes I had to end the session myself, but now when I count to ten, he stops. Then he sits up, gives me a heartwarming smile, and runs off to play with his brothers.

Now Drew is 20 months old. I try not to nurse him in public if I can help it. However, if he has a tantrum or hurts himself, I do nurse him. I have decided to let Drew wean himself. For the most part I have what I need; he's eating well, he's sleeping well, and he can spend the day away from me without a meltdown. He still needs to nurse to sleep and a couple of times during the day. He does tolerate some limitations, and if I ask him to wait a little, he usually can. I have learned that weaning doesn't necessarily happen when I think it should and that I have to remember his needs. Infancy and childhood become a fleeting memory too soon. I have learned not to rush the things that neither I nor my children are ready to give up. They will never be little again. I know I will miss the sweetness of holding a warm body in my arms while his eyes gaze up at me with the most love I have ever known.

Signs of Weaning Distress in the Mother

Engorgement or mastitis

If your breasts are engorged or you have a plugged duct or mastitis, weaning is probably going too quickly for your body to adjust. Unless there is a reason that you must wean quickly, it would be wise to slow down and allow your child to nurse more often. Mastitis and plugged ducts are greatly improved with nursing on the affected side. For your health, nurse more frequently until you are well, and then cut back on the number of nursings more slowly. Drop one daily feeding, and then wait about a week before eliminating another one.

If you must wean quickly, engorgement can be eased by expressing just enough milk to remain comfortable. Over several days, express less frequently so your milk production will gradually diminish. You should continue to drink plenty of fluids. You may find it helps to cut back on salty foods, which cause your body to retain fluids. Cold compresses on your breasts may also help diminish engorgement.

Exhaustion

Distracting a child from nursing takes quite a lot of energy. If you are on your feet all day, trying vigilantly to anticipate and avoid nursing, you are likely to be tired. If this is wearing you out or you are feeling ill and run-down, you might reconsider the wisdom of weaning just now. Continuing to nurse may well be less stressful for you than encouraging weaning. When your child is ready to wean, it will be easier.

Anger and resentment

If you're feeling angry and resentful, either because your child isn't weaning as quickly or easily as you hoped, or because you are tired of putting so much effort into weaning, it can be helpful to stop and reflect on your decision. Are you getting the results you had hoped for from weaning? Is it worth the effort? Is it feeling like a power struggle? (See "When Weaning Is a Power Struggle" below.) Anger and frustration with a prolonged weaning process are common feelings for pregnant mothers and mothers who tandem nurse. Mothers may feel this way in other weaning circumstances as well.

Try to put yourself in your child's shoes, and imagine what the weaning experience feels like for him. Sometimes our love for our children and empathy for their feelings can help us bear or overcome our own resentments. In this situation mothers sometimes decide that they will learn to live with continuing to nurse. However, if you aren't able to work through your feelings sufficiently, and the intensity of your frustration is causing difficulties in your relationship with your child, you will want to continue to find workable ways to wean. Chapter 9, "Mothers' Feelings about Weaning," has more ideas for mothers who are pregnant or tandem nursing and for mothers who for other reasons are dealing with negative feelings about nursing.

Ambivalent and guilty

Sometimes weaning doesn't go well because you are feeling uncertain about weaning. You may be wondering if weaning is the right thing to do right now, or you may be worried that it is too hard on your child. It is difficult to think clearly and make good decisions when you are feeling this way, so take some time to sort through what is happening. Chapter 9, "Mothers' Feelings about Weaning," may be helpful to you.

Overwhelmed by outside stresses

Sometimes weaning doesn't go well because there are too many other things competing for your attention and resources. If you are moving, if a loved one is ill or has recently died, if your house is being remodeled, you've started a new job, or a relative has just moved in with you, you are likely to be under stress. The list of possible contributors to stress is endless. A string of rainy days, having a cold or the flu, or having to cope with your partner working longer hours than usual can all increase your stress level. If you suspect that your energy is being used up dealing with other difficulties right now, let up a bit on your weaning plan until you feel more relaxed.

When weaning becomes a power struggle

In some situations, weaning doesn't go well because both mother and child approach it as a power struggle. Mother is going to get the child to wean, no matter what, and the child senses this and responds with equal determination not to wean. This is a tough situation to be in. Power struggles do not create the type of weaning situation where a child can be supported while she lets go of nursing.

As in all power struggles between a mother and her child, it is the mother who must take the lead in changing the situation. The best way to defuse a power struggle is to stop presenting it as such. This is easier said than done! First of all, let go of any rigidity in your weaning plans. Second, consider your child's needs and feelings. Is she really nursing more just to spite you? Or does she have a real need to nurse and connect with you? Think of how you and your child can work together. If your child is older, talk about weaning a bit and see if she has ideas about how best to wean. Sometimes defusing the power struggle by creating a partnership results in the child nursing far less, and occasionally the child may even wean.

Is Weaning Worth the Effort?

focus on what you can do to remain close, and let go of what you cannot change.

If you're reading this chapter for guidance, you have most likely already decided that weaning isn't going well and are wondering what to do now. If you must wean for a medical reason or some other reason that cannot be negotiated, it can be helpful to remember that, ultimately, what your child needs most is you. She may not be happy about weaning, but continuing to be a reassuring, loving presence in your child's life, listening to and affirming your child's feelings (even the sad and painful ones), and finding other ways to cuddle and touch will help you and your child adapt to this big change in your relationship. Focus on what you do have and what you can do to remain close, and let go of what you cannot change. Be glad for how long your nursing relationship did last. You and your child will reap the benefits for years to come.

If you do have some leeway concerning weaning, consider some other choices. Weaning should not bring distress to you or your child. You may want to discontinue weaning for awhile, even just for a couple of weeks while you re-evaluate the situation. You can also try to slow down the pace of weaning, allowing your child to nurse more often. Maybe you want to continue to encourage weaning but provide more carefully for your needs and the needs of your child. Maybe this weaning experience has taught you that you'd rather support your child in continuing to nurse until she outgrows the need than continue to struggle with weaning.

Lisa Byrd of Iowa relates why she chose to give up on encouraging weaning because of experiencing a difficult period with her son:

Like many new mothers, I believed that once a baby became a toddler, the need for nursing ended. A toddler is able to eat just about anything, so why would he need to nurse? I envisioned mothers of nursing toddlers as needy, possessive women who extended the length of time of the "normal" breastfeeding relationship to meet their own needs.

However my views changed as I nursed my son. I cherished my relationship with him as he grew into a sturdy one-year-old. Nursing helped cement our special bond, and I had no wish for the relationship to end until Scott decided he was ready.

Imagine my dismay, then, as my feelings toward nursing began to shift. On his second birthday, I became embarrassed as he tugged at my shirt in front of uncomfortable relatives. I yearned for my breasts to return to their pre-lactation state, and I longed for a little bodily privacy. I grew weary of middle-of-the-night marathons, and I sought support at every turn from my knowledgeable and kindly La Leche League Leaders. They said that if I felt the need to encourage weaning, I should gently do just that. They suggested substituting a lot of closeness, cuddles, playtime, special outings, and so on, as Scott's nursings were phased out. I set out to do so, with new birthday toys being easy distractions.

The morning after I made my decision to begin weaning Scott, he came down with a fever and a generalized case of the "fussies." I decided to postpone my course of action and settle in for a long day of lying in bed and comforting him at the breast. However, to my utter surprise, for the first time in his life, Scott refused to nurse.

I became frantic. I knew of no better way to comfort him. He would try to nurse, his little mouth encircling the nipple, but then he would pull away without attempting to suck. It was frustrating for both of us. I called our pediatrician who is a strong advocate of toddler nursing. He agreed to see us that morning.

His diagnosis was a common childhood virus that produces numerous cold sores in the mouth and on the tongue, gums, and throat. Scott was suffering a mild case, our doctor said, but he was uncomfortable to the degree that sucking was out of the question. Most of the sores were in places where the lips and tongue touched the breast during nursing.

My husband and I took our crying, hungry baby home, armed with a prescription for medicine that would numb Scott's mouth. As soon as we walked in the door, I found my breast pump and began expressing milk, planning to persuade Scott to drink it from a cup, spoon, or eyedropper.

Alas, it was not to be! Scott wanted the whole package, or none at all. He found his only comfort in putting his mouth to my breast and nestling in my arms, which helped during all but sleep times. Since birth, he'd nursed to sleep, and he was unable to be lulled without the sucking motion. I held him as he cried himself to sleep, repeating this every hour or so throughout a very long night.

The next day proved a bit better—Scott still couldn't nurse, but he was able to eat popsicles, applesauce, and sherbet. He attempted to nurse frequently, and each try was an exercise in frustration for both of us.

The sores persisted for three days, during which I pumped my milk and discarded it down the sink. The depression was overwhelming, and I was struck by the irony of the situation. I had what I had thought I wanted; Scott wasn't nursing anymore. But what a price we'd all had to pay!

Fortunately, as I write this, Scott is asleep at his father's side after nursing peacefully an hour ago. It's day five of our crisis, and the sores are gone. But the whole ordeal remains painful for all of us, and I find myself more determined than ever to allow Scott to set his own weaning timetable.

To all mothers of nursing toddlers who are thinking about weaning, my advice is: follow your heart and do what's best for your family. But first, ask yourself if ending the nursing relationship will really make things easier for you? Will it truly solve what you perceive your difficulties to be? In retrospect, I realize my frustrations centered not around nursing, but around a household that was being thrown into turmoil by visiting relatives who were pressuring me to wean. My true concern—my baby—was relegated to the background as I sought to please everyone else.

This episode drove home the point that nursing makes life much easier for all of us. It brings instant comfort, instant sleep, instant closeness after a hectic day. It's an easy answer to a two-year-old who can't make his world work the way he wants it to, and it's a haven for an overtired mother who can't stand one more minute of washing markers off the walls. It's the way we handle our crises, and it works for us.

I remember hearing a song with the lyric, "Don't it always seem to go that you don't know what you've got till it's gone?" It took almost losing our special way of life to realize how special it was, and I'm thankful it's been restored.

Help When Sudden Weaning Does Occur

It is possible that a baby or child will wean suddenly. Sometimes this is due to a nursing strike. Other times weaning happens due to a change in the family situation, an accident, or sudden illness.

Is this weaning or a nursing strike?

A baby who suddenly refuses to nurse may be on a nursing strike. If this is a baby under the age of one who is still being nourished primarily by mother's milk, you can be certain it is a nursing strike and not a natural weaning. Sometimes toddlers who have been nursing a lot cut back dramatically, and this may be a nursing strike as well. The decrease in nursing may be abrupt or take place over a few days. Two key factors that define a nursing strike are: it's sudden and unexpected, and the baby or child is unhappy. Decreased interest in nursing in a child under one may not be an actual nursing strike, but this child would also benefit from some of the following suggestions to encourage him to continue nursing a while longer.

There is usually a reason for a nursing strike, though many mothers never pinpoint the exact cause. Illness, ear infections, an injured mouth, teething, diminished milk supply, stress, or too many bottles, pacifiers, or supplements are some common culprits. Whatever the cause, a nursing strike is emotionally difficult for mothers and babies. The baby is cranky and hard to comfort, and the mother may be feeling confused, guilty, and worn-out. She may also become engorged and could get mastitis, so expressing or pumping is recommended.

There are some ways you can encourage your baby to resume nursing and end the nursing strike. One or more of the following may help:

Many mothers have found their "striking" baby will nurse when sleeping, immediately upon waking, or while dozing off.

Pumping and feeding your milk to your baby with a cup, spoon, or eyedropper will supply your baby with some of the nutrition he needs.

Offering a bottle may make your baby less likely to return to nursing.

Watch your baby's diapers and offer additional liquids if he does not have the same number of wet diapers and bowel movements as before the strike started.

Try nursing in motion, while walking, rocking, swinging, or swaying. Gently jiggle your breast in your baby's mouth.

Find a quiet, distraction-free place to nurse. Television, light, and the activity of other people may be too distracting for your baby.

Keep your baby close. Wear him in a sling or carrier, or carry him as much as possible. Sleep and nap together, bathe together (try nursing in the tub), and offer plenty of opportunities for skin-to-skin contact.

Be patient and get the support you need. As much as possible, stay home and focus on your baby.

Most of the time, a baby on a nursing strike will return to breastfeeding within two to four days, although some nursing strikes last longer. With lots of patience and persistence it is almost always possible to convince the baby to go back to nursing, so that both mother and baby can continue to enjoy its benefits. If none of the above works, after five to seven days of encouragement but no progress, perhaps your baby or child has decided to wean. See Chapter 9, "Mothers' Feelings about Weaning," for tips on adjusting to a sudden weaning.

When weaning happens abruptly

When weaning happens suddenly, the mother and child will likely both need special attention to help them adjust to the change. For the child, especially if she's distressed by the sudden weaning, much assurance of love and attention from her mother can help her to accept weaning. It can be tempting for a mother who can't nurse to distance herself from her child so she won't ask to nurse. However, this removes not only the familiarity and comfort of the breast, but also the reassurance of the mother's presence. If the mother is absent, providing consistent, loving attention from someone the child trusts and keeping a somewhat normal routine can offer some comfort.

The mother in a sudden weaning situation will need help with engorgement and preventing mastitis. She should express enough milk so that she is comfortable, but not so much that she maintains her supply. She may want to express every three hours if her baby was nursing every two, gradually expressing less often over a period of days until she no longer notices discomfort. Ice packs, wrapped in cloth, and applied to the breasts may help diminish swelling. Taking a warm shower will help ease engorgement and cause the milk to flow. Wearing a comfortable, supportive bra (maybe even a size larger) may help. The mother should drink to thirst, but may find that it helps to restrict salt intake. Binding the breasts is not recommended, and drugs that suppress milk production are not advised due to possible serious side-effects.

A mother is likely to feel sad or depressed if the weaning was sudden and she had expected to nurse longer. Finding someone to talk to who understands her grief, and spending time (when possible) with her child will help.

Children may also express grief and anger when they have been weaned suddenly. Karen J. Earle of Washington writes about helping her son through the period after his abrupt weaning:

I weaned my son for medical reasons before either he or I was ready. He is now twenty-six months old and has been weaned almost three months. I had tried to wean earlier, but without success. I found that he responded to my ambivalence and demanded to nurse more. Once I committed to weaning it became slightly easier. I say slightly easier because although he stopped asking to nurse, I had a very angry little boy for three weeks. I offered alternatives to nursing (holding, patting his back, or rocking). At first he wanted nothing to do with any of these things, and the offer of any of them only made him more angry and upset that he didn't get the "real thing."

The most important thing I learned was to allow him to grieve. It was difficult to watch my son lying on the floor, crying and screaming "No mama, no mama, don't want any mama," and to know that he couldn't accept comfort from me. I always offered comfort, but didn't insist. When he was ready, he eventually came around and asked to be held or cuddled. I let him know I was always there. Throughout the ordeal, it comforted me to know that his rejection of me and his angry expressions of hurt were those of a secure child. He knew no matter what he did, I would always love him and be there to comfort him.

Although he is now happily and successfully weaned, he still talks about nursing. When he is tired and truly wants comfort he slips his hand down my shirt to rest it on my breast. Occasionally, when he sees my breasts, he will open his mouth big, pretend he is going to nurse, then erupt into hysterical laughter at his funny joke.

chapter 11 • physical and emotional changes in mothers after weaning

When women become pregnant, their bodies begin a cycle of change. These changes continue as they give birth and then breastfeed, and the cycle is not finished until the baby is weaned. Upon weaning, if the woman is not pregnant again, her body returns to a non-pregnant, non-lactating "normal" state. Her body will be similar to the way it was before she had a child, but not quite the same.

Besides physical changes, weaning may affect a woman emotionally. She may experience unexpected changes in her feelings about herself or her child and may need time to adjust emotionally to this change in her life.

This chapter addresses some of the common physical and emotional changes mothers encounter as their babies wean from the breast. Each woman's experience is unique, and you may not notice all of these changes in yourself. Knowing what to expect will help you adjust.

Physical Changes Related to Weaning

Changes in the breasts

Women who wean suddenly may experience pain, engorgement, and leaking. In this situation, a mother will need to express enough milk to make herself comfortable in order to prevent the development of a breast infection. Abrupt weaning can be very uncomfortable for a mother. It is best to wean gradually whenever possible. (For more suggestions on preventing and treating engorgement see the section titled "When weaning happens abruptly" in Chapter 10, "When Weaning Isn't Going Well.")

Women whose babies have weaned very gradually may notice few changes in their breasts when their children finally stop nursing. Most mothers find their breasts return to their pre-pregnancy size, although the areola may remain darker than it was before pregnancy. One mother writes, "I went back to being a 34D after being a 34F or G while nursing." The Montgomery glands, which provide lubrication for the skin of the areola, may become less prominent, losing the pimply appearance they had during pregnancy. A bit of milk seems to remain in the breasts for some time after weaning. Mothers have reported expressing small amounts of milk from their breasts for weeks, months, or even years after their child has weaned.

Some mothers report that their breasts shrink, look dimpled, seem soft, or feel rather like half-empty sacks, but after several menstrual cycles, these same women report their breasts have returned to normal. Many mothers feel that their breasts are no longer as firm as they were before having their child. It's important to keep in mind that breast changes occur during pregnancy, and most women experience breast changes when they have a child, whether they nurse their babies for many months or not.

Gaining or losing weight will also affect the breasts, as will growing older. Several mothers who answered surveys for this book had been pregnant or nursing for many consecutive years, and were not certain if changes in their breasts were due to pregnancy, breastfeeding, or their own aging process.

Weight changes

There is no way to predict how any one woman's weight will change after weaning. However, if you've been able to eat heartily while nursing and still lose weight, you might safely assume that your body is using those extra calories to make milk. As your child nurses less, or you begin to wean, you may find that you can't eat the same way you have been without gaining weight. As your child weans, you will want to be aware of your decreasing caloric needs and adjust your eating habits accordingly. Of the sixty mothers surveyed for this book, eighteen percent reported gaining weight after weaning, and two gained as much as thirty pounds. (Note that this is not a scientific sampling.)

Other mothers lose weight when they wean. This may be due to lost water weight. Some mothers find they don't want to eat as much as they had been eating while nursing. Of the mothers surveyed for this book, ten percent lost weight after weaning.

When weaning is gradual, there may be no change in the mother's weight. Changes may occur earlier, when the frequency of nursing first tapers off, or the mother's appetite may naturally adapt to changes in her caloric needs.

Weight changes are also dependent on how long you've nursed, how slowly weaning happened, your age, and of course, your caloric intake and how much exercise you get.

Menstrual cycle changes

If you haven't had a menstrual cycle while nursing, you will soon resume menstruating after weaning. If your child is weaned, it is much more likely that you will ovulate without having a prior period to warn you that you are fertile. Your cycles may be somewhat irregular in the first few months after weaning. If you have nursed for several successive years, you may find that other hormonal changes related to age will affect the regularity of your period.

Emotional Changes after Weaning

Mothers experience a wide range of emotions after weaning. They vary from loss to relief, from sadness and depression to peace.

Mothers who wean gradually, or who feel that weaning happened at a time when both they and their child were ready, often feel peace and contentment when weaning is complete. When weaning happens when a mother expected it to occur, or even later than she had ever guessed she'd nurse, she often expresses more satisfaction and peace. The actual age of the child is sometimes not as important as the sense that things ended well, so mothers with children under two as well as mothers whose children are as old as four or five may all feel satisfied with the experience. Pamela Hedeman of New York writes:

When I weaned my first child at eight weeks, I experienced extreme feelings of loss and depression. I anticipated that weaning my daughter would be equally traumatic. But with absolutely no effort on my part, Juliana weaned herself at twenty-one months. I was surprised to experience a calmness and peace that assured me this was the right time. I had looked forward to a long toddler nursing period, but my "baby" decided it was time to move on. Together we entered the next phase of growing as mother and daughter.

mothers who wean gradually often feel peace and contentment when weaning is complete.

Mothers who encourage weaning and do not feel ambivalent about it may be pleased when weaning occurs. Sometimes weaning comes as a relief if the nursing relationship is a difficult one or is creating strain between mother and child. Denise Trimbach of Ohio writes:

With toddler number one, there were no limits on nursing, and the situation was out of control. She nursed every three hours, twenty-four hours a day. I nearly lost my mind. I was pregnant. My nipples hurt, but the emotional aspect was the worst part. I became very irritated during nursing and began to dread it. I turned to others for help with weaning, only to be encouraged not to do it, even though I felt it was best for my family. I needed information on weaning.

My daughter resisted all efforts to eliminate any nursings. I initiated abrupt daytime weaning, allowing her to nurse only at naptime, bedtime, and once during the night. At first, she cried when she was refused a nursing. After three or four days she didn't cry and was satisfied with substituting cuddling. My husband said he would support whatever I decided. During weaning, he often was the one to lie down with her and cuddle her instead of me. As I observed how well she dealt with an "aggressive" weaning, I was relieved and pleased. It was definitely the best decision for our family.

With toddler number two, we had limits. By fourteen months, she nursed only once during the night for a length of time I determined. She had weaned herself from daytime nursings. Before eighteen months, she had weaned herself. I was pleased to see it happen. I did not experience any feelings of loss after either weaning.

For some mothers, weaning does leave them with feelings of loss and sadness. This is a fairly common reaction. Sometimes it is due to a sense on the mother's part that the child wasn't ready to wean, but was encouraged to do so. Angela Perez-Cisneros of Tennessee writes:

With my first son, I weaned naturally and gradually. It was perfect and no strain for either of us. But with my second son, weaning was my decision. Because I was pregnant and terribly nauseous each time he suckled, I began to wean him. Even though I stretched the weaning period out over a month's time, it was still painful for us both. He wasn't really ready.

If a mother feels uncertain or unhappy about encouraging weaning, she is also likely to feel sad when weaning is complete. Sometimes weaning under these circumstances leaves feelings of regret. Several mothers in the survey for this book who pushed their children to wean continue to feel regret, including two mothers whose children are now teenagers. Bronwyn Calder of New Zealand also spent time regretting how her daughter Eleanor weaned. Eleanor was not yet one year old when Bronwyn became very ill due to pregnancy. They moved in with her mother, who encouraged Bronwyn to wean. Bronwyn writes:

Eleanor was not ready. When we first cut out night feeds she was hysterical with rage. Later she would cuddle up as she was given her bottle, and I knew she was missing something. Even now, at twenty months, only the bottle will calm her when she is really distressed.

I felt guilty, but was too busy feeling wretchedly pregnant to think about it much until Amy was born. Suddenly my guilt and grief were overwhelming. I would feed this little stranger and watch Eleanor at whatever she was doing and feel sad that our cozy one-on-one relationship was over. I was also sad that for most of the last nine months my mother had looked after her. I needed to rebuild my relationship with her, but it couldn't be the same because of the new baby.

Eleanor appears not to be too jealous of her sister. The only resentment arises when she wants me and I'm feeding Amy. She is very bright, independent, gregarious, noisy, and strong-willed. I cannot tell whether being forced off the breast affected her badly, but it doesn't seem so.

The truth is I think I had more trouble than she did. I thought I was Super Mum and could feed her as long as she and I wanted. I was angry with myself when I discovered I couldn't, and I was angry with myself for giving in and letting someone else decide on my behalf. I half-hoped Eleanor would want to start nursing again when Amy arrived. But although she shows considerable interest in the whole process, she has never progressed beyond an exploratory lick.

Amy is now three months old and writing this account has brought all the feelings to the surface again. It's easy for mothers to blame themselves (it's certainly easy for this mother), but you can only do what is best for you at the time.

In the end I put the feelings behind me because I realized I couldn't change anything and that being sad and guilty really could do Eleanor some damage. Also, I was being unfair to Amy, who is not a usurping little stranger but my beautiful little daughter who has a dimple and a very loud cry when she wants something.

I haven't stopped feeling regretful that I didn't give Eleanor the perfect start, but it was a pretty good start.

As Bronwyn points out, encouraging weaning doesn't have to mean that your child will be affected negatively forever after. And you don't need to feel you've lost touch with your child just because you've encouraged her to wean. Marcy Zimmerman of Ohio had weaned her first three children naturally. With her fourth, a medical situation made it imperative she wean her young toddler. Afterwards, Marcy commented, "Encouraging weaning was hard on me because I felt as though I was, in a way, losing my little, dependent baby. In actuality, it wasn't that way at all." Instead of harboring guilt over a less-than-ideal weaning, be comforted by remembering that you did the best you could in the situation. Vera Lynn Richardson of Ohio offers these words of comfort to mothers who have experienced some disappointment in the process of weaning:

You have given your baby a great and precious gift. You have given yourself and your milk to your baby. No one can take away that special time. Last year, when our son weaned on his own, I deeply missed our nursing relationship. However, I have come to realize that mothering is more than giving milk. Keep giving lots of hugs and kisses. Snuggling in a rocking chair may comfort your child. If you have a sling-type baby carrier, try wearing her in the sling. If you don't already share sleep with your child, you may want to consider it during this tough transition. Guilt isn't easy to cope with. Take comfort in the knowledge that you didn't choose for this to happen. Your child has been blessed with a wonderful mother who loves her and is in tune to her feelings.

Some mothers, even if they wean naturally and are planning more children, feel sadness upon weaning. Beth Lepley of Michigan writes, "About two weeks after completely weaning, I felt a great sense of loss. It was very unexpected and it even took me a little while to figure out why I was feeling that way." Ruth Penick of Ohio echoes Beth's sentiments:

No matter how long I nursed each child, I felt some sadness and a sense of loss as we reached the end of that phase of our relationship. I felt it more intensely with those who weaned at young ages and less for those who weaned when they were older. I also feel regret for the one whom I pushed to give up her last nursing time, even though she wasn't my youngest to wean.

Weaning symbolizes the end of a unique physically intimate relationship with this particular child. It is also the end of a certain type of emotional connection that naturally (and rightly) changes as a child gets older. Lori Cookson of Ohio says, "My children sought comfort in nursing. I didn't want it to end. I loved being the only one to be able to nurse and meet their needs." At the same time, weaning also teaches mothers that nursing is only one aspect of the mother-child relationship. Nancy Dumford of Ohio says, "We are still very close. I realize that nursing did not equal mothering. I am still his mother and we are still attached."

Weaning can be hard when this is your last or your only child. In this case, weaning can symbolize the closing of a chapter of your life. The period of childbearing and nursing is a unique and satisfying time for many women, and not quite like anything else we'll ever experience. And even women who remain fertile for many years after weaning their last child often feel the way Rebecca Bartlett of Vermont did when she weaned her only child: "Older!"

Sometimes weaning the last child isn't difficult, even though a mother fears it will be. Julie Cutter of Wisconsin wrote, "As Russell grew, I began dreading the thought of ever weaning him. What would it be like knowing I would never nurse a baby again?" When her son weaned, she discovered she had different feelings: "The weaning process was so gradual and painless for me this time (I remember ice packs and misery with the girls) that I found I wasn't really upset by my last baby's weaning. I knew that by letting my son lead the way, it was right for both of us."

Many mothers feel differently about each weaning with each child. Tara Rowland of North Carolina relates, "With my first child, I felt very disappointed and like a failure for weaning early. With my second child, I wished weaning had been more natural than imposed. This time, I am dealing with a sense of loss related to losing the ability to breastfeed, as well as thinking about how and when I will wean this last child."

If you are feeling sadness about weaning, it may take time to finish grieving. Allowing yourself the time to feel what you need to feel, and perhaps talking to someone who understands your feelings, will help you to get on with your life and enjoy the new stages of parenthood ahead of you. Weaning is not only an ending, but also a beginning of new adventures with your child. It can be helpful to emphasize and rejoice in what you find positive in weaning. Cyndy Glasscock of Northern Ireland writes:

My son, who is two years old, loves to nurse. I remember the first night he chose to go to sleep without nursing. He was twenty months old. I cried so hard! My husband understood that I felt a loss, but also reminded me that our son was learning to meet some of his own needs without me. I realized then that I needed to celebrate my son's growing independence, not mourn it. Although I was sad, I was also proud that he could freely choose how his needs will be met.

Missy Parkison of Tennessee offers some words of wisdom to mothers about weaning: "I believe the sense of anxiety and loss you describe is normal and natural, given the intensity and the intimacy of the breastfeeding relationship. Nursing is a special time of physical, emotional, and spiritual closeness between mother and child. However, the growing independence manifested through weaning is also normal and natural."

Life Changes

If the post-weaning period isn't going smoothly for you, it might help you to realize that you may be experiencing changes that go beyond those of weaning. As toddlers and preschoolers become school-aged children, many mothers begin to think about what they will do with their time when their children are more independent. Looking ahead like this brings choices and challenges. If you are in your forties, symptoms that you may have attributed to weaning may actually be related to perimenopause, the various physical and emotional changes that many women experience in the years before menopause. The following letter was written by La Leche League Leader Diane Beckman in reply to a question posted on the La Leche League "Ask the Experts" page which is part of a Parent Soup web site. It points out that physical and emotional symptoms after weaning are often related to aging and changes in life situations.

The question:

I've nursed my two children for a continuous seven years. My son stopped one year ago this coming November. I had a very bad two months right after he stopped, and it finally began to subside. But I still feel a lingering hormonal change, a physical lack of well-being, a tiredness and mild depression. I'm having a wicked hard time sticking to a diet which is unusual, and when I do stick to it the weight does not come off the way it used to. I'm forty-five, and I'm told I have no indication of perimenopause.

What am I asking? Are there other women out there who nursed as long as I did? What happened when they stopped? I feel the let-down response sometimes, but it is very mild. Almost like more of a memory. I would like to dialogue with anyone who has been in the same situation.

The reply:

Your question really spoke to me! I'm also the mother of two children born four-and-a-half years apart, so I also spent the good part of a decade nursing and remember the bittersweet feelings I had after my son eventually weaned. I'm interested that you associate your feelings with hormonal changes. In my case, I can separate the psychological let-down of ending that phase of my life as a mother from the hormonal changes I've become very aware of because of my long nursing experience.

Although my son weaned almost two years ago, it's only in the past year that I've noticed an increase in various symptoms associated with my period that led me to conclude that I'm indeed perimenopausal. Sometimes I think I'm reverting to adolescence with heavier periods and more intense mood changes. Like weaning, I expect this to be a very gradual process! You say you've been told that you're not perimenopausal, but you don't sound convinced. I think your emotional changes are worthy of consideration whether or not there are specific menstrual or hormonal changes. If you think you are perimenopausal, then I suspect you are right!

I can really relate to your frustration with losing weight, which I think is another sign of life in one's forties. I have found that making time in my life for two self-nurturing activities—in my case daily aerobics and piano playing, have helped me make it through my post-weaning years. Although I haven't been able to lose weight either, I know that I'm in much better shape now and I enjoy watching my fitness improve. My body just may have found the weight it wants to be!

I've been especially lucky to be one of the youngest in my aerobics class. Just as it helped to be around mothers with slightly older children when mine were babies, I enjoy hearing about life with children in their twenties. It helps me to appreciate being the mother of school-aged children who aren't too old to snuggle and need their mom.

I'm sorry that I don't have any magic answers to offer you. But I can definitely relate to the changes that accompany a happy and extended nursing existence! My best and warmest thoughts to you! May the next season of your life be as fruitful as your nursing years were.

References

Mohrbacher, N. and J. Stock. THE BREASTFEEDING ANSWER BOOK, rev. ed. Schaumburg, IL: La Leche League International, 1997.

chapter 12 · the new mother-child relationship

When a baby is born, a mother begins to breastfeed, and if she continues to nurse for many months or years, nursing becomes a major part of her relationship with her child. When nursing is over, a mother still has her child, and she still has her relationship with that child, but it is different. Nursing is no longer the means for providing security and comfort. With weaning, a mother must find other ways to fill her child's need for love.

Conveying Love and Security in New Ways

Many of the mothers who answered surveys for this book said life didn't change much when they weaned. Most of these mothers had nursed past age one or two (and many much longer) and had weaned very gradually, so many had already developed new ways to help their child go to sleep and deal with scraped knees and hurt feelings. But a child who is weaning may not have ready substitutes for nursing in place. Some children must still learn how to live happily without nursing.

Bedtime routines and night-waking

Some children who have stopped nursing still need help and support to get to sleep or to get back to sleep in the middle of the night. Many mothers and fathers establish bedtime rituals that involve reading, singing, back rubs, and reciting stories or poems. Sharon Settlemyre of Michigan writes about "parenting" her child to sleep:

At age three-and-a-half, my son still needs me to lie down with him until he's asleep at night or naptime. We transfer him to his bed and he usually sleeps through the night. If he wakes up at night, sometimes he sleeps with us, sometimes I rock him or comfort him and get him back in his bed. I try to do what he needs. We never demand he go to bed or leave him to cry it out.

Some mothers who shared sleep with their child found that weaning was a good time to introduce the child to his own bed. Others find that their child is ready to stop nursing long before he's ready to sleep on his own. Kellie Wonderly of Ohio writes, "Our daughter continued to sleep in our family bed after weaning. My husband rocked her to sleep a lot."

Sometimes weaning makes getting to sleep more difficult for awhile. Leah Morris of Washington writes, "Sleeping has been a challenge. We go for walks in the stroller at bedtime or we read more now as part of the bedtime routine. Night-waking has not been a problem since he weaned. In the morning, my son used to nurse for forty-five minutes before getting out of bed. Now we snuggle in bed."

Ann Davis of Ohio writes about how her son, Sean, learned to go to sleep without nursing:

Sean gave up nursing while I was pregnant with Jessica, because I encouraged it and because when I was about five to six months pregnant, he began to tell me that my milk tasted funny. I encouraged him to wean because holding a huge three-year-old in my pregnant lap was more than a little uncomfortable. I'm not sure how much influence I had on him, although I am sure my suggestions did decrease the frequency of nursing. But nursing was the only way he knew how to go to sleep, and both he and I were stymied as to how to replace that function of nursing. Fortunately, he understood that Mommy really wasn't enjoying our nursing relationship anymore, and Mom understood that being ready to give up nursing didn't mean Sean was ready to give up Mom.

So bedtime became a learning experience for us both. We would both go to bed early, and we would read in bed and then I would talk softly about what it was like to fall asleep by yourself. I painted mental pictures about soft and comforting thoughts. I hummed and

a child who has weaned still needs to be touched and to feel connected to her mother.

sang and told slow soft stories and talked my son to sleep. Gradually he could make these pictures himself and became very good at going to sleep on his own. I would lie down with him, and he would be asleep within fifteen minutes. Over the next few years, he could gradually go to sleep with less and less help from me: less time that I would need to lie with him, then less time that I would need to sit on the bed, then less time that I would need to be upstairs.

New ways to touch

A child who has weaned still needs to be touched and to feel intimate and connected to her mother. And mothers want to maintain closeness with their children. Lisa Albright of Pennsylvania writes, "I've found back rubs to be a nice way to touch my children affectionately, particularly my oldest, who is not a cuddly kid. This has been a good way to connect with him."

Many children find comfort and reassurance in physical contact with their mothers long after weaning. Patrice Dempsey of Maryland says of her daughter: "She enjoys skin-to-skin contact and rubbing the inside of my arm. She enjoys snuggling lying down in the spoon position, too." Some children still like to touch their mother's breast with their hand, head, or cheek. Sharon Settlemyre of Michigan says, "Our son still wants to cuddle and be held sometimes and likes to put his hand on my neck. It's a security thing for him to hold my neck and be held." Jamie Anderson of New Jersey said one of her children liked to hold her hair for security and comfort.

Parents have found many creative ways to touch their children as they grow older: "drawing" lightly with a finger on the inside of a child's lower arm or back, hugs and kisses, snuggling while reading or watching TV, and holding children (even big ones) on their laps.

Leah Morris of Washington appreciates the new ways of touching and cuddling with her child. "Before weaning, Cole would want to nurse every time he sat on my lap. Now he will sit and snuggle. I'm glad for that."

Spending time with children

Nursing guarantees a certain amount of time for mother and child to be together, and after weaning, you'll want to continue to find ways to be with your child in small and large doses. It's easy, with our busy lives, to forget to spend time regularly with our children. When you aren't sitting down several times a day to nurse, you may need to pay more attention to keeping your daily routines open for time with your child. Rebecca Bartlett of Vermont says she made a point of "staying close and doing other things at the same times of day we had nursed, so we wouldn't miss each other."

One-on-one time seems to most closely approximate the nursing experience for my sons since weaning. Taking time to do things with only one child, to talk to him a few minutes in a quiet part of the house, or to take a walk together is meaningful and connecting for both of us. This is a way for dad to "nurse," too. Carolyn Wesley of Michigan makes a special ritual of spending one-on-one time with her son: "We have 'Christopher Day' where he gets to pick what to do. I try to read and have special time with him, around the needs of my two-year-old."

The New Relationship

Children who have recently weaned may still talk fondly about nursing or even ask to nurse again after a few months. If several months have passed without nursing, few will remember how to nurse anymore. Often, it is the memories of the emotional comfort associated with nursing that children remember the best. The other day my ten-year-old son and I were talking about one of his friends who had chicken pox. He said, "I think it would be better to get chicken pox when you're little and still nursing, so you could nurse and have your mother hold you twenty-four hours a day." Weaned children are often great advocates for breastfeeding. Debra Gilley of Tennessee writes, "Barbra is now three-and-a-half years old. She thinks nursing is a way of life for mommies and our family. When Sullivan, her brother, was a newborn and would cry, Barbra would tell me to nurse him."

As children get older, they may not believe how old (or young) they were when they were weaned. Many teenagers blush at the thought of having been a nursing toddler or preschooler. Rosemary Gordon of New Zealand says, "Now at 14, he doesn't believe he really breastfed until he was seven-plus—he claims he couldn't have been any more than five!"

Weaned children often display a surprising amount of independence and initiative, even as preschoolers. In other cases, the independence takes a while to show up. Cindy Rogel of Ohio, mother of five, says this about her last child:

 He still sleeps with us, still gets up in the night, but almost always goes back to sleep, and he is with me almost constantly. But it's okay with me because of the high need of this child for security and dependence. It's who he is. He's a very touchy, affectionate little boy and continues to want to be held at the age of six-and-a-half. I feel it's important, vital, to continue to meet these needs. I am fostering independence, and he'll sprout his wings when he's ready. I have to be patient!

The mothers in the survey for this book overwhelmingly felt much love for their weaned children and felt close to them. The bond of nursing seems to last long after the physical act of nursing is gone. As Connie Mesco of New Jersey writes, "I feel I know her inside-out because of the close bond nursing gave us." Liz Koch of California writes:

I believe it is the long, nurturing relationship—the deep bonding— that keeps my kids still wanting to be around and helps me to put up with all the rest of what parenting involves. When my daughter is abusive verbally I call upon my deep connection to her to help me rise to the occasion and struggle to communicate with her and help her find the tools to help herself.

Closeness takes on many forms as children grow. Mary Frier Swisher of Michigan writes:

Although they have all gone (and are still going) through the normal pulling away, we are quite close. My twenty-year-old often calls from college just to talk (on her own bill, mind you!); my six-foot, sixteen- year-old son still waits for his hug and kiss every morning before leaving for school (and often hugs me back!), and my eleven-year-old still likes to cuddle (sometimes!).

For mothers, nursing is the one thing we can do for our child that no one else can. Losing that special connection is often poignant for mothers. Bonnie Weinberg of Israel expressed it this way: "Our relationship is now a regular relationship, like the one he has with his father or grandmother. I'm no longer the only one who can comfort or console him. It's a relief but also a bit sad."

For many mothers, breastfeeding led to an emphasis on togetherness, even after weaning. Kathy Maier of Pennsylvania writes: "We're very close. We're a tight-knit family, and do everything together."

Mothers often feel that nursing and meeting the needs of their children when they are little creates trust that lasts a lifetime. Leah Morris of Washington says, "I feel trusted to listen to and meet Cole's needs." Breastfeeding and weaning also teach mothers to trust their children.

Looking Ahead

Weaning is one of the many "letting-go's" mothers experience with their children over the years. With weaning we can practice letting go with grace, having confidence in our children and trusting in their ability to grow and thrive. Mothers of older children say that other times for letting go aren't any easier and that it is always hard to see our children need us less. But at the same time, it feels good to see children grow into the independent people we want them to be and to know we have played a part in this process. Ann Lahrson of Oregon writes:

What I had feared might turn out to be an empty, sad stage—the weaning of my baby—is turning out to be a delightful turning point in our path through life together. New exciting ways of relating to one another are gradually replacing the old comfortable ways. It feels good to reflect and realize that, as in any relationship, we must either grow or stagnate, and Erin and I are movin' on!

Many mothers feel that their breastfeeding experiences have shaped them as mothers and have changed their attitudes about mothering in a permanent and lasting way. Maria Sara Villa of Colombia writes eloquently about this:

 The nourishing continues beyond weaning. Breastfeeding, with all the tenderness, the communication, the compromise, and the devotion to one's children, "programs" us for a family life full of those values. I believe that it gives us attitudes that we can use in so many other areas. It makes us more loving in discipline. It makes us be more present for our children. And they return the abundance of love that we feel.

Life is different in little ways, too, after weaning. Sue McGough of Minnesota writes about anticipating life after weaning:

 "Mama, Mama." Then a long pause. Maybe he went back to sleep. "Mama, want nee-nee!" It's Dane, my two-year-old, with his 3:00 AM wake-up call. I slide over to his bed and get my pillows arranged. He cuddles up with a contented sigh, his warm feet tucked up against me. These nighttime nursings have always been a special time, but lately I find myself cherishing these moments even more. I recently have begun to realize that soon I won't be nursing anyone anymore. Dane is our third and (sigh) last child. As this special season of life draws to a close, I have been asking and answering questions such as:

Will I miss nursing? Yes, and no.

Will I lift my shirt instinctively when someone lies in "that" position? Probably.

Will my breasts shrink? My husband hopes not.

Will I finally be able to wear one-piece outfits and belts again? Yes!

Will I go jogging and discover I've left one flap down? No!

Will I be glad that I chose to take the time to nurse these little people so long? Absolutely.

A final thought on weaning, and life after, is expressed in this poem by Barb Haskell of Washington:

SWEET FAREWELL

I never knew
In the beginning
The immeasurable effect
  our times together
Would have upon my heart
Emotions
The strong cords of love
That wrapped themselves
  around and round my body
Soul
Spirit
While cradling you
  warm at my breast
Ageless
Ancient
Present
Future
Stronger than any element
  within the scope of the
  Universe
Complex
Yet so simplistic
  it took my breath away
Mother sustaining baby
Heart to heart
Warm and soft
How oceans of feelings
  swept over me
Sweet tide of intimacy
Pulling me ever deeper
  into the underworld of
  magical motherhood
Fathomless
This love we shared
Mother and child
Protector Provider
Innocent Depender
Numbered
Those days of rarest
  pleasure
The tide must turn
As always it will
The day I had not wanted
Ever

To imagine
Came
No more my role
  as intimate sustainer
Complete comforter
You have blossomed
Grown outside of those
  sweet sweet stolen
  moments of delight
My heart aches
  with tender memories
Even while rejoicing in your
  budding independence
My arms long to hold you
Within the safe cocoon
  of my love
Even while wisely letting
  you go
Butterfly that you have
  become
The tide is inevitable
Much as I would have
At times
Desired to hold it back
The course you must follow
  is a natural one
In good time
All things must cease
But how unexpected
This anguish mingled
  joy of motherhood
How unutterable the sorrow
  of loss
The pain of longing for days
just barely ripe with time
My spirit soars
  with deepest gratefulness
For those moments we shared
For no tide can sweep them
  away from me now
Because of you
I am left
In the end
A much altered soul

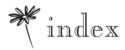

index

La Leche League International is a nonprofit organization founded in 1956 by seven women who wanted to help other mothers learn about breast-feeding. Currently, there are La Leche League Leaders and Groups in countries all over the world.

La Leche League offers information and encouragement primarily through personal help to those women who want to breastfeed their babies. A Health Advisory Council comprised of medical consultants from all over the world offers advice and assistance when necessary.

La Leche League is the world's largest resource for breastfeeding and related information, distributing more than three million publications each year. THE WOMANLY ART OF BREASTFEEDING, a basic how-to-book, has helped countless mothers through almost any nursing crisis. Other books published by La Leche League, including MOTHERING YOUR NURSING TODDLER by Norma Jane Bumgarner, are sold in bookstores and through the LLLI mail order catalogue.

For further information, we urge you to locate a La Leche League Group in your area by checking your local telephone book or by calling 1-800-LA-LECHE in the USA (800-665-4324 in Canada) or by writing to LLLI, P. O. 4079, Schaumburg, IL 60168-4079 USA (LLLC , 18C Industrial Drive, Box 29, Chesterville, Ontario, Canada). Or you can visit our web site at www.lalecheleague.org /